FUNDS
FOR THE
FUTURE

FUNDS FOR THE FUTURE

Report of

The Twentieth Century Fund Task Force on
College and University Endowment Policy

Background paper by
J. PETER WILLIAMSON

McGraw-Hill Book Company

New York   St. Louis   San Francisco   London   Düsseldorf
Kuala Lumpur   Mexico   Montreal   Panama   São Paulo
Sydney   Toronto   New Delhi   Singapore

THE TWENTIETH CENTURY FUND is a research foundation engaged in policy-oriented studies of economic, political, and social issues and institutions. It was founded in 1919 by Edward A. Filene, who made a series of gifts that now constitute the fund's assets.

Library of Congress Cataloging in Publication Data

Twentieth Century Fund. Task Force on College and University
    Endowment Policy.
    Funds for the future.

    Includes bibliographical references.
    1. Universities and colleges—United States—Finance.
I. Williamson, John Peter.   II. Title.
LB2342.T85 1975   379'.1214'0973   75-34378

ISBN 0-07-065620-7 (paperback)
ISBN 0-07-065619-3 (hard cover)

Contents

Foreword

The nation's private colleges and universities have long since gained recognition for their remarkable achievements—winning academic freedom, providing scholarship aid to needy students, and bringing to American higher education a diversity and a flexibility that are unmatched anywhere in the world. But today, these institutions are in trouble.

During the tumultuous years of the last decade, many campuses were beset by problems that were largely the result of rapid growth. The post-Sputnik enthusiasm for higher education combined with the baby boom and student deferments to bring about great expansion in educational institutions, both public and private, and simultaneously to provoke student—and faculty—discontent with some university policies, decisions, and practices.

At the same time, the great bull market of the 1960s lured many colleges and universities to adopt aggressive investment policies. But following the debacle in the stock market, many institutions that had seen large profits turn into severe losses became conservative, forsaking growth for income. Institutional expansion gave way to retrenchment and perhaps even decline. Today, the object of student protests, when they are taking place, is university budget cuts. And many informed people seriously question the ability of private institutions of higher education to survive.

Convinced that private colleges and universities represent a vital national resource and concerned about the demographic, economic, and financial difficulties already apparent, the trustees of the Twentieth Century Fund decided to assemble an independent Task Force to consider and report on the controversial and significant issue of endowment policy.

The distinguished authorities named to the Task Force believed wholeheartedly in the importance of preserving private colleges and universities and developed a sense of mission about how best to pursue this objective. Rather than concentrating solely on the management of endowments, they chose to examine endowment policy in a broad context. They gave considerable attention to the need for active programs to build endowments and to integrate endowment policy with spending policy. They also emphasized the importance of improving disclosure policies, so that all those persons interested in the prospects of such institutions can understand their plight and measure their progress.

The dedicated commitment of all the members of the Task Force has resulted in a Report that affirms their faith in the future of higher education. This document provides a series of thoughtful, integrated recommendations that, while addressed primarily to trustees who are ultimately responsible for their institutions, can be read with profit by everyone concerned about strengthening the financial foundations of private colleges and universities. The Report is accompanied by a comprehensive background paper by J. Peter Williamson, who is a professor of business administration at the Amos Tuck School of Business Administration, Dartmouth College, and a consultant to The Common Fund. His paper greatly assisted the Task Force in its deliberations and provides a wealth of factual information on the critical issues of endowment policy.

We at the fund are grateful to the entire Task Force, all of whom contributed to the discussion and the formulation of recommendations. I must make special mention of John Gilligan, the chairman of the Task Force, who not only presided with wit and grace at its meetings but also became imbued with the necessity of bringing a broad perspective to the examination of endowment policy. At the last session of the Task Force, he told his colleagues that their labors together had proved an invaluable learning experience for him, one that deepened his awareness of the role played by private colleges and universities in fostering the essential values of our society. I am confident that the Report of the Task Force will be just such a learning experience for all of its readers.

M. J. Rossant, DIRECTOR
The Twentieth Century Fund
September 1975

Members of the Task Force

Report of the Task Force

INTRODUCTION

For higher education, the 1960s were years of prosperity. Although campuses experienced considerable turmoil, it was not of a financial nature. Degree-credit enrollments surged from 3.5 million to 7.5 million. State and federal spending on higher education more than quadrupled, increasing from $2.2 billion to $10.4 billion. Classrooms were filled as quickly as they could be constructed, and rising costs were easily passed along to students or taxpayers. The Carnegie Commission on Higher Education accurately described the decade as "the golden age" of higher education.

In contrast, the past few years have witnessed an abrupt end to painless growth for the nation's private colleges and universities. Overall, enrollments have been stabilizing, costs have been rising, and endowments, as a result of a steep decline in the markets, have been depressed. In early 1975, the Carnegie Foundation for the Advancement of Teaching predicted that financial difficulties would force one of every ten private American colleges to shut down, merge, or consolidate within the next five years.

Boom, of course, does not have to be followed by bust, but the financial pressures on private institutions have become increasingly severe in the changed and more perilous environment of the past few years. More and more schools are operating at a deficit, despite the best efforts of their trustees and administrators. Many have recognized the need to take fresh and strenuous action to cope with the problems that now beset their schools. Yet the basic difficulties—lagging enrollments, rising competition for students, increasing costs, and a growing gap in tuition charges between public and private institutions—are not likely to disappear.

This Task Force believes that the survival of many private colleges and universities is now at stake. Even the strongest and wealthiest institutions cannot prosper without effective long-range plans to deal with the new and difficult conditions that prevail. These plans must provide for the creation, the management, and the proper utilization of endowment. In this Report, we have focused on endowment policy, because we regard it as a particularly troubled and controversial area.

In the booming stock market of the 1950s and 1960s, the potential value of endowment became dramatically evident. During the 15 years ending June 30, 1965, the rise in stock prices as measured by the Standard & Poor's Composite Index averaged 11.0 percent a year. Even when adjusted for inflation by the Consumer Price Index, the "real" rise was 8.9 percent a year.

But from June 1965 through June 1974, the Standard & Poor's Index of 500 Common Stocks rose at an annual rate of only 0.2 percent, and in real terms the stock market actually declined 4.5 percent a year. An equities endowment of $100 million that had fared as well as the stock market did would have declined, over this period, to $66 million in terms of purchasing power. Although a few endowments may have managed to do better than the average, the performance data that are available suggest that most performed worse, with holdings of both equities and fixed-income securities suffering sizable losses. Table 1 shows the course of stock and bond markets over the 25 calendar years 1050–74.

These disappointing results, so shattering to expectations, coupled with an increased awareness of what endowment can mean to an institution, have led trustees and administrators to search for answers to some fundamental questions about their endowment

Table 1   Total Return, Stocks and Bonds* 1950–74

	STOCKS		BONDS	
YEARS	"NOMINAL" COMPOUND ANNUAL RETURN (%)†	"REAL" COMPOUND ANNUAL RETURN (%)‡	"NOMINAL" COMPOUND ANNUAL RETURN (%)†	"REAL" COMPOUND ANNUAL RETURN (%)‡
1950–54	23.7	20.8	2.3	−0.2
1955–59	14.9	13.1	−0.5	−2.1
1960–64	10.7	9.3	5.6	4.3
1965–69	4.9	1.5	−2.9	−6.2
1970–74	−2.3	−7.9	6.7	0.6

*Total return includes price changes, dividends, and interest.
†Nominal returns are based on the Standard & Poor's Index of 500 Common Stocks and on bond indexes maintained by Salomon Brothers, as reported in Ibbotson and Sinquefield, "Stocks, Bonds, Bills and Inflation: The Past and the Future," Center for Research in Security Prices, Graduate School of Business, University of Chicago, 1974.
‡Real returns are nominal returns adjusted by the Consumer Price Index.

funds: What should be the investment objectives of the endowment? Who should manage it? How can an institution be assured that its endowment fund is well managed? And what is an appropriate spending policy? Recent advances in the theory of investment management shed new light on these critical questions, although it is safe to say that there are no sure or simple answers.

The Task Force recognizes the hazards in attempting to set out specific recommendations. Institutional needs and resources differ; no set of policies can be universally satisfactory, and no magic formulas are available for solving the financial problems of institutions of higher learning. Colleges and universities are exceedingly complex institutions, and this complexity is reflected in differences in planning, decision making, and reporting. Nevertheless, the Task Force hopes that its recommendations, and the accompanying background paper by J. Peter Williamson, professor of business administration at the Amos Tuck School of Dartmouth College, will be a source of ideas and insights useful to trustees and administrators in undertaking an examination of their own policies and will help them to frame their own principles for the effective use and management of endowment funds. *The Task Force believes that the challenges of recent years should impel boards of trustees at every institution to reevaluate, conscientiously and systematically, long-range objectives, management, development, and spending policies for endowment.*

PRESERVING PRIVATE INSTITUTIONS

The Task Force believes that the preservation and strengthening of the nation's private colleges and universities are essential to the public interest.

A large number of authoritative studies have documented the contributions of private institutions to higher education and the value of higher education to the nation. Clearly, the quality of our higher education—the variety of academic programs and the range of choices available to students with widely different interests, aptitudes, and financial resources—is unequaled in any other country. Much of this richness stems from private institutions, which for many years were almost the only institutions of higher education in the United States and which remain unique sources of academic strength.

But pressures brought about by the acceleration of inflation, along with the shrinkage in the purchasing power of endowments, have placed private institutions in critical financial difficulties. Survival alone presents a serious challenge to many of them.

Endowment funds form a key element in the preservation of private institutions.* They provide a stable, long-term source of income to support educational programs and to offer financial aid, through scholarship assistance and other forms of help, for students.

The appropriate level of endowment varies from institution to institution, and the trustees of each institution must determine their own needs and goals. Ideally, the Task Force recommends that, at a minimum, the endowment of a private institution should enable it to keep its tuition close enough to that of public institutions so that it can continue to attract qualified students. It recognizes, however, that measured by this standard, the endowments of most private institutions are too small.

Public support for private higher education is also necessary. The Task Force urges increased public support of private institutions by means that preserve their independence and the diversity that serves the public interest. This support should include incentives for the development of endowment capital, such as the tax deductibility of contributions, along with programs to supplement the use of endowment for meeting such expenses as direct student financial assistance and the renovation and replacement of existing physical facilities.

This is not a case of special pleading, because public support for private institutions will not entail an added drain on the resources devoted to higher education. On the contrary, it will help to conserve them. With the nation facing the prospect of slower growth in higher education and perhaps ultimately a decline in total enrollments, legislators must recognize that it makes little sense, either economically or educationally, to seek to provide higher education facilities or programs that duplicate those already available in the private sector. Nor does it make sense to stand by passively while private institutions founder. If private institutions are allowed to perish, these services will inevitably have to be provided by public institutions whose funding will be drawn primarily from the public treasury.

In a period of uncertainty characterized by a marked decline in the rate of growth, both public and private institutions must make more constructive efforts to avoid wasteful competition. Since few private institutions are now in a position to think in terms of expansion, the issue arises only in the public sector. Legislatures and the governing boards of public institutions should undertake expansion

---

*The term "endowment funds," as used by the Task Force, refers to all the earning assets of a college or university, whether or not they fall within the narrow legal definition of "true endowment."

and the construction of new facilities only after careful study demonstrates a vital need for additional educational capacity. All those directly concerned with the well-being of private institutions should make themselves aware of pending state and federal policy proposals dealing with higher education and urge responsible action on their legislators.

RESPONSIBILITIES OF THE BOARD OF TRUSTEES

Service on the board of trustees of a college or university is a significant social responsibility. It requires a special commitment to—and an intimate involvement in—the affairs and objectives of the institution.

Trustees, of course, do not directly manage a college or university. But they hold the ultimate responsibility for the institution—for its physical plant, personnel and student body, instructional resources, administration, operating budgets, development, endowment, and relations with the outside world. The exercise of responsibility calls for planning, control, and the selection and evaluation of management. Planning begins with identification of the institution's mission. It goes on to the setting of objectives or standards for the academic, financial, and other activities of the institution, against which the trustees can judge the accomplishments of those to whom management has been delegated. Accordingly, trustees must require from administrators all of the information necessary to ensure that they have a thorough understanding of the institution's financial affairs, which is essential for making these judgments.

Trustees generally are conscientious in financial planning, at least in the short run. The current budget is likely to be the subject of a good deal of thought and scrutiny. Normally, short-run financial objectives are set out rather precisely. These areas often receive attention at the expense of nonfinancial objectives and long-run financial objectives. Yet one important responsibility of trustees is the best possible allocation of resources between present and future generations.

The Task Force recommends that every institution develop a long-range plan (covering at least five years) that reconciles revenues and expenditures for current operations and for capital improvements. The plan should include enrollment expectations, academic programs, salary levels, operating costs, investment management, and development efforts and projected construction. Planning must take into consideration the indications that college and university enrollments will level off and decline in the 1970s and 1980s and examine the implications of this decline for tuition revenue, for operating expenditures, and for the role of endowment.

Obviously, drawing up a plan is a meaningless exercise unless effective implementation of the plan is possible. So it is critical to see to it that what is planned can, with effort, come to pass. Under present circumstances, moreover, an effective plan, one that achieves consistency, will probably call for the reallocation of resources. In many cases, it will involve reducing expenditures, making greater efforts to attract gifts, and improving the investment return of the endowment fund. All this is easier said than done; yet responsibility consists in large part of facing up to hard realities and exhibiting a determination to deal successfully with them.

Because the Task Force has been especially concerned with the performance of endowments, it is appropriate at this juncture to point out that past approaches may have lost their validity under present realities. *Specifically, the Task Force is convinced that the tradition of defensive custodianship of an endowment fund is no longer in itself an adequate exercise of trustee responsibility.* Such a narrow approach can make a well-preserved endowment the sole monument to a defunct institution. Some of the legal constraints that have imposed on trustees a preoccupation with the preservation of endowment funds, rather than their management for the overall benefit of the institution, have been modified in recent years; conscientious trustees can find opportunities to use endowment effectively in meeting the overall needs of an institution even within the most restrictive legal framework.

In general, planning can be improved by paying more attention to the procedures and structures involved in the operation. Most boards of trustees will find it useful, if not essential, to form small committees (whose dedication can be relied on) to study vital areas of institutional management and to develop policy recommendations about them for the board as a whole. The special skills and knowledge required for service on such committees ought to be considered when seeking new trustees.

Financial planning is one of the vital areas of institutional management. The formulation of an overall long-term plan is ordinarily a responsibility of the finance committee; if it does not take on this assignment, some other committee must do so. The finance (or budget) committee also should be charged with responsibility for drawing up the spending policy for the endowment. But the major tasks involved directly with the endowment call for other committees.

Accordingly, the Task Force recommends the formation of a development committee, which would have specific responsibility for building the endowment, and an investment committee, which would have specific responsibility for supervision of its performance.

ENDOWMENT BUILDING

Since endowment is so vital to an institution, *the Task Force urges that trustees undertake a concerted and aggressive effort to assure its development through systematic and effective fund raising.* Even at the richest institutions, the investment return on endowment funds will almost certainly not provide adequate institutional support in the foreseeable future. Moreover, higher education must increasingly compete for public funds with other urgent or critical needs that may well receive a higher priority from state and federal legislators. Consequently, the development effort required to build endowment must take on greater significance than ever before.

It is the view of the Task Force that fund raising is so important that every board of trustees must establish a development committee. The members of the development committee should compare the fund-raising performance of their institution with that of other comparable institutions and develop a broad-based plan for improvement. However, the main job of the committee should be increasing the awareness of the need for support among the natural constituency of the institution—its students, parents, alumni, and all others with an interest in or an obligation to see to its continued well-being. Efforts should be made to expand that constituency by familiarizing alumni and friends with the current programs and activities of the institution. When appropriate, deans, faculty members, and others in the academic community should be enlisted in fund-raising efforts.

A high degree of professional ability is required to mount and carry out long-term development campaigns. Therefore, a development officer who ranks as a key member of the president's staff and who, preferably, devotes full time to fund raising should work closely with the development committee. In evaluating performance, the Task Force recommends that expenditures for development be judged by their long-run productivity rather than by standards of expenditure or requirements for economy in other areas.

Development officers can succeed in obtaining contributions to the endowment only if they have confidence in the management of the endowment and are skilled at explaining its objectives to potential donors. So it may therefore be appropriate for the development officer to sit in, from time to time, on meetings of the investment committee.

The development committee and trustees generally must resist the temptation to emphasize gifts for current operations or for program expansion at the expense of the building of endowment. A well-drawn fund-raising plan will strike an appropriate balance between short-term operating needs and long-term needs for capital. It may require some imagination to persuade donors to support the general endowment rather than the construction of new buildings bearing their names, but in the years ahead, survival is more likely to rest on the former than on the latter.

Institutions also should be imaginative in seeking out forms of giving that will appeal to donors in varied circumstances. For example, deferred giving, through life annuities, life income trusts, and bequests, ought to be part of the development program. Although it does not meet immediate needs, the option of deferred giving may prove extremely productive and serve to maintain needed endowment growth.

The income and estate tax deductibility of gifts and bequests to colleges and universities has made it possible for individuals, estates, trusts, and corporations to provide greater support for higher education than they would otherwise have given. These deductions have contributed to an enormous growth in private support of higher education (from around $240 million in 1949–50 to over $2 billion in 1973–74). Today, the need for private support is greater than ever.

The Task Force believes that because private institutions are in the public interest, it is in the public interest to encourage gifts to them. We urge trustees to take the responsibility for efforts in the public arena that may be needed to protect incentives for gifts to higher education. It has become evident in recent years that superficially plausible efforts at tax reform could have devastating consequences for institutions that depend upon charitable gifts. At the same time, prudence requires that an institution avoid opportunistic and questionable practices (abusing its tax-exempt privileges, for example, or promoting tax gimmicks for donors) that provoke public retaliation or loss of donor confidence.*

---

*For further discussion of development activities, see Chapter I and Appendix 1 of the background paper.

ENDOWMENT MANAGEMENT

Responsibility for the endowment lies with the trustees. Those who give the institution their financial support and those who depend upon the institution for their education or livelihood are entitled to hold the trustees accountable for the productivity of its resources.

Whatever the size of the endowment, the trustees should appoint an investment committee, separate in function from the finance committee and composed of not less than three nor generally more than six members, whose regular attendance at meetings can be counted on. Although some of the members of the committee may be specially qualified nontrustees, a majority should be trustees and the chairman should be a trustee. One individual (or more) familiar with the management of securities portfolios should be included. In addition, one or more executive members of the administration, preferably the president or treasurer, should also attend meetings in an ex officio capacity. *To maintain reasonable continuity and to ensure that no single individual will dominate the committee, the Task Force recommends that all members be appointed for staggered limited terms.*

The Task Force strongly urges that deliberate and vigorous steps be taken to avoid any real or apparent conflicts of interest in investment management. Conflicts may arise if officers of the institution's bank, broker, or investment manager sit on the investment committee. Although the institution may occasionally benefit from business transacted with a trustee, the full board should be aware of the relationship and must supervise it carefully to avoid embarrassment to the trustees and to the institution itself.

To strengthen its deliberations, the investment committee should be provided with part- or full-time staff. The staff should work closely with the committee, particularly with its chairman, preparing reports, analyzing the performance of the endowment, monitoring investment management and custodial costs, reviewing cash management procedures, and performing other essential tasks that are too often neglected. Many institutions could achieve regular and substantial savings through closer control of their custodial arrangements and their cash balances.*

The primary functions of the investment committee are to recommend to the board a set of investment objectives, to select profes-

---

*This topic is discussed in detail in Appendix 1 of the background paper.

sional management, to determine with the manager the appropriate degree of managerial discretion within the limits of the objectives, and to evaluate the manager's performance.

Perhaps the committee's most difficult assignment will be to establish and quantify investment objectives. All too frequently, trustees select an objective such as "maximum total return (income plus appreciation)" or "the highest and most stable income that can be achieved without excessive risk and with due regard to preserving capital in a period of inflation." Such statements of conflicting goals, undefined terms, and vague platitudes are no substitute for a set of measurable objectives.

The Task Force believes that the trustees should require and approve a written set of objectives for the endowment fund and assure themselves, at regular intervals, that these objectives remain valid and are being pursued. The investment objectives should incorporate expected return and limits on risk and volatility, expressed in terms of limits on investment strategy. * These limits should be detailed and specific; they should include appropriate ranges for the stock/bond ratio, volatility, diversification, stock and bond quality, and portfolio turnover. A majority of the Task Force also favors the inclusion of a minimum earned income requirement—that is, a specified level of dividend and interest income. Finally, the committee should provide an estimate of long-run total return and the probable long-run growth of the endowment.

The full board should review the committee's statement of objectives at least once a year. When long-run expectations change, the committee should recommend modification of these objectives.

The Task Force believes that, over the long run, equities and equity-related investments will provide greater returns in real terms than will bonds or other fixed-income investments. Yet few institutions can tolerate for their entire endowment the extent of volatility frequently experienced by the stock market. Since it is our view that market volatility is likely to continue at or near recent levels, we caution against an extremely aggressive policy of investing solely in common stocks. Such a policy invites a costly overreaction, with panicky trustees shifting to bonds or other fixed-income securities at the bottom of a stock market decline.

But we do not advise a policy of extreme conservatism. An insistence on stability will almost certainly result in a heavy sacrifice in long-run investment return. Moreover, it also is likely to bring about a dangerous reaction of the opposite sort, with trustees shifting into stocks at the top of a rise when the investment climate is at its most euphoric.

*Chapter II of the background paper discusses investment objectives in some detail, and Appendix 2 contains examples of statements of objectives.

    Instead, the Task Force recommends that trustees agree on a range for the proportions of stocks and bonds, with a clear understanding in advance of what an extreme drop in the market will mean to the overall value of the endowment. A cash-equivalent reserve may be appropriate to meet liquidity needs, depending upon the probable flow of income and of gifts and the amount the institution has decided to spend from endowment.

    Although investment risk is a concept that defies precise definition, the Task Force believes that in establishing investment objectives for an endowment, it is useful to consider two kinds of risk. The first is exposure to permanent capital losses due to the misfortunes of an enterprise in which the endowment has invested. A bankruptcy, for example, may bring about this kind of loss. The damage to an endowment can be reduced by diversification and maintenance of quality standards for stocks and bonds. However, both the board and the investment committee should be primarily concerned with the overall risk of loss to the portfolio rather than with the safety of each individual bond or stock.

    The second kind of risk is "market risk," the risk that the value of a fund will fluctuate with the securities markets. The only protection against this risk is to invest in securities with lower volatility.

    Stocks and bonds are the traditional investments of endowment funds and will continue to be so for most institutions. But the investment committee should be aware of opportunities in other kinds of assets. These other investment media, which include real estate, oil and gas properties, and mortgages as well as stock lending and option writing, have their own risks and usually demand special management skills. The Task Force believes that institutions should never invest in such opportunities without competent counsel, but it urges trustees to find or develop this competence where the fund is large enough to achieve the necessary diversification.*

    The Task Force believes that the full board, assisted by a special committee it may designate, should make all major policy decisions on social responsibility issues. Although the investment committee should advise the board on the financial implications of any social responsibility decision, the board, not the committee, should deter-

---

*Hans Jenny states:
    The total range of investment alternatives goes beyond the confines of the endowment. For instance, plant debt may cause a net cash outflow that is greater than the total long-run return on endowment investment. Similarly, the net total return resulting from added "marketing" dollars to, for example, admissions or development, may far exceed the return associated with endowment investment. Ultimately—within the confines of legal requirements—it is the total return not of the endowment fund, but of the sum total of institutional assets that should be considered by trustees.

mine the institution's policy. The chairman of the committee might
assume responsibility for the voting of proxies.*

*The Task Force believes that skilled professional management is essential
for all endowments. Trustees should leave the day-to-day management of the
endowment, including the selection of securities for purchase or sale, to the
manager.* Internal management of the endowment is a sensible choice
for only the very few endowments that are large enough to pay for all
the services required to manage an endowment effectively. Most institutions should turn to outside investment managers. In our view,
professional management over the long run will outperform non-
professional management, but a substantial body of data casts doubt
on the ability of any professional manager to outperform the market
consistently, even allowing for the particular limitations imposed by
an institution's investment policy.

A critical aspect of selecting a manager is matching the manager's
investment philosophy and style with the objectives of the institution.
The manager also must be prepared to give the time and effort that
are necessary to produce satisfactory results for the institution. There
is not much to be gained by comparing the historical performance
records of potential investment managers as a means of choosing an
investment manager. At best, performance records are only a rough
guide; many investment managers with the best records in a rising
market did poorly in a falling market.

*Thus, the Task Force feels strongly that common purpose and compatible
investment philosophies are the most important criteria for selecting the appropriate manager. A specialist in market timing, for example, is clearly inappropriate as a manager if the committee has decided not to take the considerable
risks associated with market timing. Past performance statistics should be used*

---

*Roger Murray states:
This proposal for dealing with social responsibility issues arising in connection with
portfolio investments is, in my opinion, unrealistic in view of the time pressures normally at work. The investment committee—or a special committee appointed for that
purpose—must be in a position to act expeditiously between board meetings. Even with
the assistance of extensive background data from an organization such as the Investor
Responsibility Research Center, reaching timely decisions on complicated questions is
extremely difficult.

The investment committee members are constantly passing upon proxy questions
of a business and financial nature with which social responsibility issues are inevitably
mingled. They should be free to act for the board but required to report annually and
to review board policy positions with the full board and perhaps other interested
groups.

Messrs. Dilworth, Eastburn, Jenny, and Porter wish to be associated with this
statement. *Mr. Eastburn adds:*
The concept of social responsibility should also include the investment behavior
pursued by the investment committee. In the past, uncritical adoption of current investment fads as they have come and gone has at times undoubtedly contributed to unsound
conditions in financial markets. The investment committee has a responsibility to avoid
such activity.

only with great care, and trustees seeking managers who will outperform the stock market should fully understand the risks of doing so.

The manager will, of course, be expected to pursue the institution's investment objectives, but it is up to the investment committee to decide just how much discretion to grant him. A manager, for example, may have developed a strong stomach for extensive swings in the market, but the committee may want to limit his—and its— exposure to gain or surprise. So each committee must make this decision for itself; the wider the discretion the greater the gain if the manager is successful, and the greater the loss if he is not.

Institutions with large endowments (over $25 million) may want to achieve their objectives by diversifying investment style through the use of more than one manager. This approach, though, can be expensive in terms of higher fees, added time, and other costs. Most professional managers who have achieved any success maintain an investment philosophy that is consistent over time. Managers who switch their philosophy as conditions change are apt to do worse. So the use of several managers with different approaches, each following his own individual approach consistently over time, offers the prospect of attractive diversification. For smaller funds, the Task Force recommends the use of a single manager for common stocks and bonds, one whose investment approach shows strength in diversification rather than specialization.

In reviewing potential outside investment advisers, most trustees will probably consider The Common Fund—a pooled fund established in 1971 to permit endowment funds, particularly those of smaller institutions—to obtain the advantages of professional management. The Task Force believes that trustees should evaluate The Common Fund like any other manager, on the basis of the similarity of its objectives to those of the institution. In particular, trustees should be aware that its assets are invested almost entirely in common stocks and that it therefore bears a higher risk than a fund with a significant percentage of bonds; so it is likely to be appropriate for only a portion of the institution's funds.

The Task Force recommends two kinds of manager evaluation, one long term and one short term. *The investment committee should evaluate the manager's performance in terms of rate of return over at least a full market cycle. The return should be compared to a standard (or standards) agreed upon in advance, a standard comparable in terms of risk and other constraints to the formal investment objectives of the endowment.* In principle, a "risk-adjusted" rate of return should be computed for evaluation purposes, but in practice, this computation can prove difficult. A variety of comparable indices and averages is probably the best basis for comparison. The endowment performance data collected annu-

for comparison. The endowment performance data collected annually by the National Association of College and University Business Officers furnish an increasingly useful base for comparisons. *The Task Force also urges that trustees look to the total return of the endowment in evaluating its performance. Artificial distinctions between "income" and "principal" serve only to make evaluation and decision making more difficult.*

The committee also should monitor frequently the manager's success in achieving the agreed-upon objectives. If the manager fails to meet the objectives, the committee should fully understand the reason. Quite apart from his statistical record of performance, the committee should be sensitive to inconsistencies in the manager's approach and to signs that he has lost confidence in his own strategy. A high rate of return is no guarantee that objectives are being met, nor is a low return over a short time period necessarily an indication of poor management.*

FORMULATING SPENDING POLICY

The allocation of resources between current and future generations is another major responsibility of the board of trustees. In determining the annual distribution from the endowment, trustees should recognize both the current needs of the institution and the importance of reinvestment of earnings to meet future needs.

Establishing a spending policy begins with an understanding of three important aspects of the endowment's operation. The first is the investment process, which produces income and appreciation. The second is the spending of all or a part of this income and appreciation for the institution's benefit. The third is the spending rule or formula that relates the second to the first.

For true endowment funds, the law has traditionally permitted the spending of income only (dividends, interest, and the like). Such a rule has left its mark on the investment strategy of a number of institutions in the form of a minimum-yield requirement. Other institutions have devised a different rule for "quasi endowment"—endowment not subject to the strict legal limitations governing true endowment—a rule permitting the spending of a portion of apprecia-

---

*For additional material on the management of the endowment fund, see Chapters II, III, and IV of the background paper.

tion as well as income. Still other institutions, particularly those in states that have adopted the new Uniform Management of Institutional Funds Act, apply this "yield and gain" spending rule to both true and quasi endowment. This spending rule generally leaves investment strategy free of a yield requirement, permitting that strategy to focus on "total return."

No matter what spending rule is followed, the trustees must establish the *level* of spending that they consider both appropriate and prudent. After estimating the probable long-run total return the endowment will achieve, the probable rate of endowment growth due to gifts, and the probable rate of inflation in the institution's costs, this exercise requires a determination of what portion of the total return, over the long run, should be spent. This decision should be made, and ratified, by the full board. Short-run investment results should not be allowed to have a major effect on spending.

The Task Force believes that if spending from endowment consistently exceeds 5 percent of the total market value of the endowment, too little of the total return is being reinvested for the future, and the value of the endowment will not keep pace with the nation's rate of inflation. In our view, 5 percent of total value—not a return based on equities alone—is a reasonable figure for a benchmark, based on historic rates of inflation and total portfolio return. Some evidence suggests that inflation in the costs of higher education has generally been two to three percentage points higher than inflation in the nation generally. Thus, just to keep pace with its own inflation rate, an institution should be striving for endowment growth of at least 2 percent a year through gifts and limiting average spending to no more than 5 percent of market value.

Whether or not the spending rule permits spending of a portion of appreciation as well as income, it must be consistent with the investment strategy and spending needs of the institution. Stability in spending from year to year, an important goal for most institutions, can be achieved through a conservative investment strategy designed to produce a stable combination of income and appreciation or through a spending policy that will convert a more aggressive investment strategy, and therefore more variable investment results, into stable spending. If the first course is followed, the result is likely to be slower growth in the endowment. If the second, the emphasis on higher growth may result in much more variable performance from one year to the next, so that a firm spending rule will be required to assure a stable return.

The Task Force maintains that spending needs should not dictate investment policy nor investment policy dictate conditions of spending. But trustees must be satisfied that the investment policy, the spending rule or policy, and the *projected spending levels are consistent and achieve a balance between the present and future needs of the institution.**

Requiring that the endowment produce an income sufficient to cover planned spending (without expenditure of appreciation) may impose a discipline on the manager to limit investment risk. In view of the difficulties of defining and limiting risk, most members of the Task Force believe that such a requirement may be useful, although limiting risk can be accomplished in other ways.†

The members of the Task Force agree that investment objectives must include appropriate limitations on risk and that an institution that does not impose a yield demand on its endowment must find alternative constraints. Finally, in recognizing the usefulness of a "yield-only" spending policy as one of several devices for limiting investment risk, the Task Force does not (in the absence of legal prohibition) oppose spending a portion of appreciation from the endowment.‡

*Hans Jenny states:
To arrive at a consistent set of guidelines governing investment policies, spending rule, and long-range expenditure levels is among the most difficult tasks required of trustees. The conflict between budget requirements and long-term endowment investment policy is real and will not soon disappear. Therefore, my preference would be that investment and spending policies converge in a manner designed to smooth the impact over time on the operating account. High volatility in market values should not become a reason for program retrenchment that makes the institution less attractive to future generations of students.

†Roger Murray states:
Those of us who do not consider this method useful believe that greatly superior approaches to the control of risk characteristic now exist. We believe that a yield-only spending policy may be positively harmful to investment management, because it creates an artificial pressure to maximize current yield rather than the total productivity of the investment alternative.

Messrs. Banks, Dilworth, Jenny, and Porter wish to be associated with this statement.

Robert Augsburger states:
Since endowment returns (income and appreciation) are relied upon to support on-going, long-term program commitments, there must be a reasonable expectation that the level of spending can be achieved year in and year out. Out of two sources of returns, dividends and interest are most stable and reliable on a short-term basis, while appreciation is unstable and unreliable on a short-term or year-to-year basis. An endowment fund can accept year-to-year volatility of principal, but it should not accept volatility of income. Consequently, whatever level of spending or spending rule is adopted, the principal component of the amount to be spent should be derived from earned income (dividends, interest, rents) with this being supplemented, when necessary, by appreciation to achieve the desired level of spending. For this reason, investment objectives should contain a minimum-earned-income requirement as an additional restriction. Such a requirement is no more harmful to investment management than are constraints such as the stock/bond ratio, diversification, volatility, and quality. In fact, income (and growth of income) is the primary goal of investment management, and it should take precedence over and perhaps be the determining factor in formulating other investment objectives.

Messrs. Cabot and Putnam wish to be associated with Mr. Augsburger's statement except for the admonition that earned income should be supplemented, when necessary, by appreciation in order to achieve desired spending levels.

‡Spending policies are discussed in detail in Chapter VI of the background paper.

FINANCIAL AND ENDOWMENT REPORTING

The financial reporting of a college or university serves a number of major institutional needs: it permits the trustees themselves to plan sensibly on the basis of their institution's financial position; it enables faculty and students to understand the plans made; and it facilitates the development effort. To be effective, such reporting must go well beyond the standard financial statements now prescribed for colleges and universities.

The Task Force recommends that trustees develop a program for regularly communicating the financial position and needs of their institution—including the status and performance of the endowment—to alumni and other potential supporters, as well as to faculty and students and other members of the institutional community. Trustees also should take steps to gauge the reaction of alumni and others on the effectiveness of the information that is being disseminated.

If gifts are to continue to build the endowment, then donors must have confidence in the way in which the institution manages its funds. The Task Force recommends that all institutions report the status and performance of their endowment funds in understandable terms, employing, wherever possible, unit values, unit income figures, and references to other comparable funds.* The board of trustees should assure itself that the performance of the endowment is being accurately measured.†

CONCLUSION

The days of wine and roses, as New York's Governor Hugh Carey stated in another context, are over. So is it with private higher educa-

---

*The recent publication of the investment committee of the National Association of College and University Business Officers, entitled *Reporting on Investments of Endowment Funds,* is a good source of suggestions for the preparation of readable and useful reports. For additional material on financial and endowment reporting, see Chapter VI of the background paper.

†*Hans Jenny states:*
Although some additional expense and certain technical difficulties may arise, it would add to the objectivity of such reports, if periodically—every three or four years—an independent "audit" were required by the trustees on the manner in which performance is estimated and reported.

tion. Now and in the decade ahead, private higher education will confront, among other problems, declining enrollments, a growing gap in tuition charges of private and public institutions, and extreme difficulty in achieving productivity increases.

Students, faculty, and many administrators may naturally be more concerned with the immediate needs of their college or university than with its long-range future. But trustees have the responsibility to consider not only the institution's present priorities but also its long-range goals and prospects. In the past, when higher education was booming, trustees could often ignore this obligation. Now and in the future, trustees who fail to establish a set of long-range objectives and develop a sound plan for achieving them may place their institution in jeopardy.

Although trustees are responsible for all the operations of the university, their involvement in its financial affairs is particularly important. This Task Force began to examine better management of endowment funds as a way of easing some of the financial strains on private higher education; it soon realized that endowment management, important as it is for many private institutions, is best viewed as one element of the institution's total financial management and cannot be expected by itself to provide needed solutions to financial problems. Consequently, although this report focuses on the problems of endowment management, we have sought to stress the importance of developing and planning efforts in order to bring wider considerations to bear in meeting the problems of the next decade.

This report is directed primarily to trustees, because they will, in large part, determine the future of private higher education. But its recommendations are important for administration, faculty, and alumni as well, and trustees should seek the support of these groups in assuring that vigorous attention is given to the problems that lie ahead.

Private higher education has played a central role in American society. The Task Force believes that it can—and must—continue to do so. The essential task of trustees, as the Task Force sees it, is to place their institutions in a sound educational and financial position to meet the challenges and exploit the opportunities they will confront in the years to come.

Background Paper

By J. Peter Williamson

ACKNOWLEDGMENT

For the helpful comments and suggestions of a great many people, I am grateful. I shall not attempt to name all the brokers, money managers, consultants, accountants, lawyers, foundation officers, and college and university trustees and financial officers who have helped. But I must express special thanks to the members of the Task Force, who patiently read early drafts of the background paper and offered their suggestions. And I owe a particular debt of gratitude to George F. Keane, Executive Director of The Common Fund, for his very careful review of my chapters and the benefit of his enormous experience of the world of endowment funds. Finally, to my secretary, Eunice Ballam, my renewed thanks for care and patience in dealing with endless and excruciating detail.

J. Peter Williamson
Hanover, New Hampshire
August 1975

Introduction

After two decades of relative prosperity, colleges and universities are now facing critical financial problems. Higher education is confronted with the harsh reality of both a slowdown in enrollments and a continuing rise in costs. What is more, the prospect of an actual decline in enrollment appears imminent. Although it is still too early to tell whether the quality of higher education will ultimately be strengthened or weakened by these developments, it is clear that the premises and policies appropriate in an era of rapid growth are inappropriate for an era of slowdown and uncertainty.

One aspect of higher education that deserves fresh scrutiny is the college or university endowment. During the late 1960s, many institutions came to regard their endowment funds as an increasingly important source of educational funding. The spectacular rise in the stock market during the 1950s and early 1960s led to widespread optimism about the contribution that endowment funds might make to the financing of higher education. The subsequent decline of the market has been a source of considerable anguish.

THE VALUE OF PRIVATE HIGHER EDUCATION

Since private colleges and universities lean more heavily on endowment fund revenues than do public institutions to support their operations, this study is primarily concerned with private higher education, which, for many years, was the dominant form of postsecondary schooling in the United States. In recent years, however, public higher education has been expanding, a development that not only has made life more difficult for private institutions but has also led some to question whether they are as essential as they once were.

The evidence available should convince the skeptics. Every recent study of higher education has endorsed the importance of private higher education. For example, the 1973 Report of the National Commission on the Financing of Postsecondary Education identified three objectives for higher education that are well served by private institutions. The first is student access:

> Each individual should be able to enroll in some form of post-secondary education appropriate to that person's needs, capability and motivation.[1]

The second objective sounds an even clearer call for private institutions:

> Postsecondary education should offer programs of formal instruction and other learning opportunities and engage in research and public service of sufficient diversity to be responsive to the changing needs of individuals and society.

Although it would be a mistake to regard private institutions as uniquely "independent" and therefore superior, since no institution, public or private, is truly independent of all outside influences, the differences between the dependencies of public and private institutions are what is significant. Both are subject to pressures, some good and some bad, from outside and from inside. But the pressures differ, and these dissimilarities assure the distinctive contribution of private institutions to higher education.[2]

The National Commission included institutional independence as the third special value of private institutions:

> Institutions of postsecondary education should have sufficient freedom and flexibility to maintain institutional and professional integrity and to meet creatively and responsibly their educational goals.

If private institutions are to provide a variety of choice, diversity, and institutional independence, it is obvious that they must be financially secure and not overly dependent on revenues from any one source. This goal would not be easy to achieve even in good times; but in a period when the financial prospects for private higher education seem so uncertain and the temptation to turn to government sources of revenues so great, it becomes even more difficult. Endowment funds, however, offer a much needed source of revenue to private institutions, one largely free of outside influence, and thus are likely to play an increasingly important role in the prospects and planning of private institutions.

THE FINANCIAL ENVIRONMENT

An enormous volume of material on the seriousness of the financial condition of private higher education clearly confirms that it is experiencing an atmosphere of "crisis."[3]

One measure of the serious financial difficulties that many colleges and universities have encountered in recent years lies in statistics on closings of institutions. The National Commission reported that there were few closings until 1967–68; then the number rose rapidly, reaching a high of 44 in 1971–72. There was a decline, however, to 29 in 1972–73 and to only 2 in 1973–74.[4]

Most of the institutions closing down were private. The National Commission's report found the prospect for private colleges and universities much worse than that for public institutions, in part because of the "tuition gap." Private tuition averages from three to five times the tuition for public four-year colleges and universities, and the difference is growing.[5] In terms of net tuition charges, that is, net of financial aid to students, the gap per student grew from $302 in 1953–54 to $967 by 1969–70 for universities, from $295 to $900 for four-year colleges, and from $249 to $782 for two-year colleges. The Carnegie Commission concluded that the widening gap is responsible for a decline in the share of total enrollment held by private institutions.[6] In an article published in 1972, a future increase is projected and a prophecy put forward that private education may soon be pricing itself out of the market.[7]

THE IMPORTANCE OF THE ENDOWMENT RESOURCE

Endowments do not provide an adequate financial base for many schools. William Jellema's studies of the financial problems of private institutions provide data on the size of endowments.[8] The average endowment assets per full-time student ranged from $1130 for the "largest" institutions (over 4,000 students) to $2360 for the "small" institutions (500 to 1,000 students), suggesting that the average income contribution per student made by the endowment is very low. Thus, even for the small colleges, assuming a return/yield of 5 percent, endowment is contributing on average less than $120 per year per student. The ratio of endowment income to total income for colleges and universities has been declining for a long time and may now be close to stabilizing at this admittedly low level. In 1900, endowment accounted for 25 percent of educational income; by 1928–30,

Table 1   **Sources of Educational Income—Public and Private**
Institutions

| | *1969–74* | |
SOURCES OF EDUCATIONAL INCOME	PUBLIC INSTITUTIONS (%)	PRIVATE INSTITUTIONS (%)
State & local government	68	2
Federal government	12	13
Tuition & fees	17	59
Endowment income	1	9
Gifts	3	17
Total educational income	100	100

Source: Carnegie Commission on Higher Education, *Higher Education : Who Pays? Who Benefits? Who Should Pay?* (New York, N.Y.: McGraw-Hill Book Company, 1973), Tables 4 and E-1.

the contribution was down to 12 percent; and by 1956–57, it was only 5 percent.[9] A recent study of a group of private four-year liberal arts colleges shows that the percentage contribution of the endowment to educational and general income dropped during the decade ending 1969–70 for 37 of the colleges. Only 10 showed an increase.[10]

Although the steady fall in contributions from endowments has been offset to some extent by a rise in gifts for current use, the total contribution made by endowments and current gifts has also declined. In 1915, the combined contribution accounted for 24 percent of educational income; by 1958, it was only about 13 percent.[11] The Report of the National Commission on the Financing of Postsecondary Education noted a continued decline for the five years ending 1971–72.[12] A similar conclusion can be drawn from Figure 1, which shows that for private institutions the aggregate contribution has declined from about 41 percent in 1929–30 to about 26 percent in 1970–71 and is projected to drop to about 20 percent in 1983.

THE TASK AHEAD

In strict financial terms, these statistics suggest that endowment funds are becoming less important to colleges and universities. Potentially, however, the role of endowment funds is becoming increasingly significant. For one thing, endowments provide a way for private colleges and universities to diminish the gap between their tuition and the tuition charged by public institutions. For another, because endowment funds are under the control of the institutions themselves, they offer trustees an opportunity to experiment and innovate largely

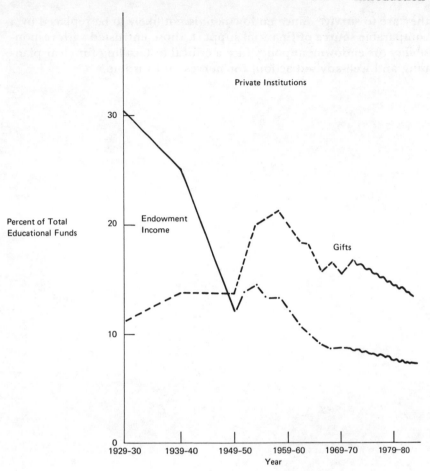

Private Institutions

Percent of Total
Educational Funds

30

20 — Endowment
Income

Gifts

10

0
1929–30   1939–40   1949–50   1959–60   1969–70   1979–80
Year

Source: Carnegie Commission Report, Tables A1–A13, 3, and E-1.

Figure 1. Endowment Income and Gifts as a Percent of Total Educational Funds

independent of outside influences. Finally, as the financial pressures on private education intensify, every source of funds becomes absolutely critical.

For these reasons, then, endowment funds will be called upon to play a critical role in private universities and colleges during the next decade. Whether they will succeed is largely up to the trustees of each private institution. Even the best-endowed institutions face financial difficulties; many others will have to develop their endowments if they are to survive. Since endowment is not likely to be replaced by a comparable source of financial support, those entrusted with responsibility for endowment policy face a critical test, calling for clear planning and well-advised action, for nerves and wisdom.

I/Overall Financial Planning and the College or University Endowment

Most trustees are all too familiar with the tendency of boards to become bogged down in administrative detail. This chapter begins with a plea for much better planning than can now be found at most colleges and universities. The following conclusions, based on a study of the boards at 19 state colleges and universities, should remind trustees of the need for a firm resolve to stick to important issues:

> The most significant finding of this research is that the boards undertake a tremendous volume of decision actions in the course of a year's meetings, and much of this volume is in the form of pro-forma actions on long lists of detailed operational matters. The responsibility for legislative policy formation, long-term planning, administrative guidance, review of performance, and support of the institution as it faces hostile critics from within and without the campus is frequently given minor attention or left to the initiative of administrators or governmental agencies.
>
> • • •
>
> The preoccupation of most boards with excessive amounts of operational detail is further illustrated by the fact that the largest proportion of nearly every board's actions, in some cases a majority, were in the lowest level category of policy implications. . . . Sixty percent of all decision items came to the boards with a recommendation for board action, and another 30 percent came in reports or lists without recommended action specified. Only 4.6 percent of all board actions originated in an independent motion of a trustee.[1]

Planning is, after all, the key to survival. Planning begins with overall goals, which clearly have financial implications, and therefore must go on to financial planning and to specific consideration of the endowment.

Most experienced trustees are familiar with at least some planning of current operations. What is rare, however, is a plan that incorporates capital assets as well as current operations and brings about consistency between the development and maintenance of capital resources and the progress of current operations.

INSTITUTIONAL GOALS AND FINANCIAL CONSEQUENCES

For almost every institution, several cost relationships are of critical importance. In higher education, there is no history of steady productivity increases and no reason to expect significant productivity increases in the future. During this century, output per man hour, the usual measure of productivity, has increased at about 2.5 percent a year in the economy in general. This means that wages generally rise about 2.5 percent a year without costs of production, and therefore prices, rising. Wages in higher education will probably rise about as fast as wages in other parts of the economy, but since there is no increase in output per man hour, costs of production rise just as much. Even in the absence of a general inflation in prices then, we can expect the salary and wage cost component of higher education to rise at about 2.5 percent a year. Since wages do not account for all of the costs of educational institutions, total costs will rise a little less than 2.5 percent. This is not necessarily a devastating prospect. The wage earner will find that the cost of education is simply keeping pace with his wages (the higher-priced institutions, of course, may be moving farther out of his reach). But education becomes 2.5 percent more expensive every year *relative to other goods and services.* And one might expect that over time this shift in relative cost may affect the choices people make between higher education and other goods and services.

Price inflation is a fact of life, and wages increase somewhat more than 2.5 percent a year. But whatever the rate of price inflation, this 2.5 percent differential, or some percentage close to it, will separate the increase in the cost of education from the increase in the cost of goods and services where productivity is effective. The differential has not been constant over the year. In the 1960s, when it reached 4 to 8 percent at a number of institutions, in part because academic salaries were making up the ground they had lost during World War II and the early post-war years. A Carnegie Commission Report has urged that at a minimum higher education get back to the 2.5 percent differential.[2] Indeed, the report presents a number of reasons for bringing the differential below 2.5 percent, perhaps by making "one-shot" economies at an institution, thus reducing the differential for a year. But this is very different from a permanent reduction. In 1971, Earl Cheit estimated that a "minimum-growth" policy for higher education in the early 1970s would involve a 4 percent differential, while a "rock-bottom" policy would involve a 1 percent differential.[3]

The most recent information on inflation in higher education, developed by Richard Wynn, shows that for a 20-college sample inflation in educational and general expenses over the decade ending in 1973 was about 1.6 times the inflation measured by the Consumer Price Index.[4] Since the Consumer Price Index rose by an average 3.2 percent a year over the decade, the expenses of the colleges rose at an average 4.8 percent, and the differential was 1.6 percent. This apparently modest differential results in part from the fact that, as Wynn concluded, labor-related expenses constitute about 75 percent of the educational and general expenses of a liberal arts college. So a productivity differential of 2.5 percent should translate into a total cost differential of three-quarters of this, or about 1.9 percent for a liberal arts college. This, as a matter of fact, is exactly the differential reported by the Carnegie Commission Report for the period 1953–54 to 1966–67.[5] As Wynn points out, there may be some reason to expect the differential to narrow in the near future, because the rate of increase in academic salaries is once again dropping below the rate of increase in wages and salaries generally. But this probably means that in the longer run there will be another "catching up," and therefore an increase in the differential.[6]

These numbers provide some rough guidelines and more indications of what trustees might expect at their own institutions. They also suggest, as Wynn urges, that it may be a good idea for trustees to keep track of the rate of inflation at their own institutions and compare it to inflation generally.[7]

The "quality" of an institution, which is not necessarily the same as its reputation, and for which there do not seem to be any generally accepted objective standards, is probably a major feature of overall planning at any college or university. Trustees will have some intuitive feel for the quality of their own institution and the need for maintaining or improving it. For example, a low ratio of students to faculty is frequently taken as an indication of superior quality. Beardsley Ruml said in 1959 that this idea is "sheer fantasy,"[8] but the Carnegie Commission Report cites evidence that there is a strong relationship between the student/faculty ratio and the quality of an institution. The report does go on to point out that student/faculty ratios are frequently the result of chance rather than planning.[9] So it may be well worth considering Ruml's suggestion that the student/faculty ratio could be increased at a number of institutions with no loss of quality.

The Carnegie Report refers to a study of 12 colleges that reveals wide differences in costs per student not necessarily related to differences in quality.[10] Indeed, the report suggests that costs are very much the result of revenues and that cost differences among institutions are as likely as not to reflect no more than the differing abilities of those institutions to attract income.[11] So economies are probably possible in most institutions, without a sacrifice of quality. (By 1975, of course, many institutions had already cut their budgets substantially.) The Carnegie Commission Report expressed the belief that for higher education in general the cost per student could be reduced 1 percent a year during the 1970s—a total of 10 percent by 1980.[12] The report specifically suggested more restraint both in administrative expenses and in expenditures for student services.[13]

Recognizing possible opportunities for economy and bringing those economies about are, however, not the same thing. The Carnegie Report had some useful suggestions that mostly had to do with rewarding departments for cost savings,[14] for establishing incentives within an institution to bring about economy.

The trustees of any institution are forced into allocation choices among the major activities of an institution, including instruction, research, and public service. Within these major activities, there are departments, professional schools, centers, and programs, and at a still lower level, there is the array of courses offered. Some activities are clearly much more expensive than others.[15]

Choices among activities for the institution are particularly important if the instittion faces a probable slowing in the growth of enrollment or even an enrollment decline.

Closely related to choices among possible activities for the institution are those related to capital improvement and expansion. Every trustee must be well aware by now of the permanent increase in costs associated with new facilities. But in the past, a number of institutions seem to have willingly accepted gifts of new buildings and other facilities without much concern for the costs of future maintenance. The Carnegie Report recommends that departmental budgets include a charge for rent so that the trustees may see just where the carrying costs of a new facility will show up in the institution's current operations,[16] and whether or not rent is charged, it may well be time for institutions to begin charging depreciation as an expense. A funded depreciation reserve could serve as a source of financing for renovations, which are becoming more common than new buildings. Alternatively, if renovations are financed by borrowing (even by borrowing from endowment), the entire debt service could be charged as an expense analogous to depreciation.

Determining the appropriate size and the rate of growth of an institution is a key part of the overall strategy that the trustees must develop. More than one institution has been dismayed when a strategy geared to a particular growth rate has failed badly because growth did not meet expectations. The generally high growth rates into the late 1960s were quite helpful for public institutions, whose budgets rose as legislatures recognized the need to build and staff. A recent leveling off has brought hardship to institutions that were geared for permanent growth. For private institutions, growth may have been less beneficial, although it has probably stimulated a good deal of private philanthropy and will have made possible easy expansion of faculty and casual proliferation of activities. The Carnegie Report suggests that some small colleges may *have* to expand in the future, simply to reach a viable size.[17]

One of the most important constraints facing higher education is the probable decline in growth in regular enrollment through the 1970s, with an actual shrinkage in enrollments in the mid 1980s.[18] This process is based upon what is *known* with regard to the college age population in future years and what is *expected* with regard to how many will actually choose to go to a college or university. The trustees of a particular institution may have a different forecast for their own enrollment, but they cannot afford to ignore what is going on in the nation as a whole. If nothing else, we can anticipate greater competition in the attraction of students in the 1970s and particularly in the 1980s.

Some particularly interesting suggestions for dealing with the slowdown and decline are suggested by Kenneth Boulding, who feels that educational administrators have generally experienced rapid institutional growth and were presumably chosen for their skills in coping with growth conditions, but that now a new set of skills may be needed and perhaps a new group of administrators.[19] Boulding refers to good and bad examples of coping with decline at the secondary and elementary school level and to some moderate successes and outright disasters in the industrial world. An interesting conclusion is that there are opportunities for the improvement of quality in the midst of decline.

It may be time not only to consider the likelihood of a leveling off or a decline but also to prepare, even as something to be held in reserve, a strategy to deal with decline.

In 1959, Beardsley Ruml suggested some specific questions for the trustees of liberal arts colleges to consider in developing an overall strategy for the institution. For the most part, they have not lost their pertinence:

- Does it appear that this institution will be able to compete for high-quality faculty and students over the next 10 years, when competition for both will be increasingly severe?
- Is the college now able to compete on favorable terms with state universities and strong private institutions for the most promising young teachers? Is it able to retain the experienced teachers it wishes to keep?
- Is the college now able to attract all of the qualified students it can accommodate? If not, is this situation of recent origin, or some years' standing? . . . What proportion of a class graduates four years after entering college? How much of the attrition is caused by academic failure?
- Do the answers to these questions indicate that the institution's position is stable, improving or deteriorating? . . . is the institution now of an economic size?
- What is the average number of students per teacher? How many courses are offered each semester? What are the enrollments in these courses? . . . How many classes have fewer than 5 students? Between 5 and 10 students? And so on, up to the largest class? . . . Are there significant differences among the departments? Are there special courses or programs which do not attract many students but which the college maintains because it has established a reputation in the field?[20]

Ruml was dealing with private liberal arts colleges, and he was writing to the trustees with respect to their own individual institutions. The Carnegie Report addressed itself to the problems of higher education in general, and its recommendations were directed to the nation at large rather than to the trustees of a particular institution. Still, the specific nature of some of these recommendations makes them useful to the trustee thinking of his or her own institution. Here are some suggestions for achieving financial savings:

- Halting creation of any new Ph.D. programs except under very special circumstances . . . achieving minimum effective size for campuses now below such size; and for departments within campuses, particularly at the graduate level . . . moving toward year-round operation so that more students can move through the same capital facilities . . . cautiously raising the student-faculty ratio . . . reexamining the faculty reaching load.
- Improving management by better selection and training of middle management, by giving more expert assistance to the college president, and by improving the budgetary process.
- Establishing consortia among institutions; and also merging some.

But the report cautioned:

- We consider it unwise, however tempting in the short-run, to cut such items as: necessary maintenance; library expenditures for new books and for journals; student aid, without at least making loans available.
- We also consider it unwise to keep down costs by excessive turnover of low-paid assistant professors.[21]

FINANCIAL PLANNING

For every set of overall goals and strategy, there is a corresponding set of financial goals and strategy, and the trustees must be sure that the sets are consistent. As a practical matter, the device for establishing the financial goals to accompany a set of overall goals is a long-term budget—a projection of revenues and expenditures for at least 5 years, and hopefully for 5 to 10 years, and an accompanying projection of capital resources. It is this projection that conveys in dollars and cents just how the overall goals will be implemented.

Projections of expenditures will depend upon expectations of enrollment; changes in programs; upgrading of quality in different parts of the institution; shifts in emphasis among educational, research, and other activities; and, of course, inflation. Projected tuition will depend upon enrollment expectations and the rate of tuition increase. Net tuition revenue will depend upon plans for financial aid. Anticipated foundation grants and government support may be significant, especially if research activities are substantial. Gift revenue may be very much a function of the trustees' commitment to development efforts. And expected revenue from endowment will depend upon the investment committee's choice of an investment policy.

The usual role of endowment is to furnish a continuous and growing contribution to the budget of an institution. Spending from endowment is customarily gauged to bring about a rate of growth in the contribution which keeps pace with inflation. A trustee may want to consider how well this conventional wisdom fits the needs of his or her institution. Perhaps the strength of the institution would be better served by heavy current spending from endowment in order to make a major impact on quality of facilities or on educational programs. Or perhaps it would be better served by spending very little currently, saving toward the period of declining enrollment that can be foreseen for a decade hence.

In most institutions, the financial officers will prepare projections, but the trustees have the final responsibility for seeing that these projections are consistent with the overall goals of the institution and that they are realistic. Richard Wynn, in his study of inflation in higher education, points out first that projections should reflect the inflation inherent in higher education rather than price inflation generally.[22] And while it may be useful to develop some inflation statistics for a particular institution, in order to make better judgments about its probable future rate of inflation, Wynn suggests going even further and identifying significant differences in inflation among different programs and departments of a single institution.

The ultimate in financial projections is the use of simulation models. Stanford University is one institution that has developed models for making financial forecasts under a variety of conditions.[23] Other models in general use include the Resource Requirement Prediction Model of the Western Interstate Commission on Higher Education; the SEARCH model of Peat, Marwick, and Mitchell; and CAMPUS, a model prepared by Systems Research Group. The human mind simply cannot cope intuitively with the interrelationships of all the financial aspects of a college or university and all the consequences of change. Even a very simple computerized model can be of great value, and, indeed, simple models have often proven more successful than complex models because they are more readily understood.

THE ENDOWMENT FUND

Expectations of the endowment fund's contribution are an important part of any financial planning. However, the term "endowment" covers a variety of funds among which there are quite important distinctions for legal purposes as well as for purposes of devising investment objectives and meeting fund-raising goals.

The first distinction is a legal one, between "true" and "quasi" endowment (meaning "funds functioning" as endowment). True endowment funds represent funds that have been given to an institution on the condition that the principal is to be preserved, with income (dividends, interest and the like) used to support the institution's activities. There are various forms of language that may identify a gift as being for true endowment, and often it is difficult, in reviewing the terms of gifts made long ago, to determine exactly what was intended.[24] The language is obviously important for separating true endowment, for which the principal must be kept intact, from quasi endowment, from which principal may legally be spent. And for institutions in the 16 states that have adopted the Uniform Management of Institutional Funds Act, it is also important in determining whether, even for true endowment, a portion of appreciation may be spent in addition to income yield. The Uniform Act permits this for true endowment funds unless the terms of the gift explicitly forbid it.[25]

Some gifts establish "term endowment," subject to an explicit condition that principal be kept intact only for a period of years. Such a gift constitutes true endowment until the condition lapses; it then becomes quasi endowment. And some gifts of true endowment are accompanied by a requirement that income from the gift be added to principal and not spent for a period of years.

In general, quasi endowment represents funds that the trustees of an institution have decided to treat as permanent capital, although they are not legally obliged to do so. Some quasi endowment is the result of gifts that come free of explicit limitation against spending principal (although the donors may have expected this result); some represents the addition to endowment from operating surpluses during good years; and some is a portion of endowment income to establish reserves against a possible decline in that income.

Quasi endowment is a particularly valuable resource, which can serve to meet emergency needs, and is especially useful in the application of spending formulas that involve the potential spending of more than income yield.

The distinction between true and quasi endowment is essentially a legal one, but at some institutions the distinction seems to extend to investment policy. Some boards of trustees seem willing to invest quasi-endowment funds more aggressively, at greater risk, than true endowment funds. If an institution makes use of a spending formula that prescribes spending a planned percentage of market value, the proportion of quasi endowment in the total endowment fund may be quite important in determining the kind of investment policy that is compatible with the spending formula.

The terms "restricted" and "unrestricted" are occasionally incorrectly used as synonyms for "true" and "quasi" endowment. "Restricted" properly refers not to whether principal may legally be invaded but to the use to which spending may be applied, regardless of whether that spending includes income only or both income and principal. A gift to be used exclusively to support a rare book collection constitutes restricted endowment. If the gift is also one of true endowment, then the principal must be kept intact. If it is not, then principal may legally be spent. But, in either case, the spending may be used only for the restricted purpose—support of the collection.

A narrow restriction on the use of endowment may present serious problems if the gift is a large one and the activity becomes relatively unimportant to the institution and no longer merits any spending. But broad restrictions, such as limitation to the support of a library, are unlikely to present any difficulty so long as the total library budget exceeds the spending from endowment restricted to library support.

Annuity and life income funds (or "deferred gifts") are rather specialized kinds of endowment (see Appendix 1). A gift annuity is a blending of both a gift to a college or university and the purchase of an annuity. The donor makes a payment to the institution, which in turn undertakes to pay to him, or to others, an annuity for life. The payment is calculated to finance the annuity and to leave a residual gift to the institution. Gift annuities can fit the financial needs of some donors extremely well and attract funds that are unlikely to come in the form of ordinary outright gifts. Some institutions, particularly on the West Coast, have built up very substantial gift annuity programs. Pomona College is probably the outstanding example. Eastern institutions were slower to start but have shown a growing interest in recent years in gift annuities.

Life income trusts fulfill the same general purpose as gift annuities. The beneficiaries of the income trust receive the income earned on a gift, and on the death of the last beneficiary of a trust, the principal is transferred to general endowment. The gift element in the establishment of an income trust is generally larger than in the case of an annuity.

Life income funds are not available to support the institution—not even income is available—until the income beneficiaries under a particular income trust have all died. At this point, the residual value attributable to the particular trust becomes true endowment and can contribute income to the institution. Annuity funds need not be kept separate, except to the extent that state laws require the maintenance of identified reserves, but they usually are.

POOLED AND SEPARATE FUNDS

When an institution receives a gift to be added to its endowment, it is always possible to establish a "separately invested" fund for that gift. The separate portfolio of stocks, bonds, and perhaps other assets needs management and bookkeeping distinct from that of other endowment funds. Some institutions still have a great many separately invested funds, but in recent years, the high cost of maintaining separate funds has led to a tendency to merge as many as possible into one or more common pools.

A merged, or pooled, endowment is rather like a bank common trust fund. A particular gift, when it is received, is added to the pool and is credited with units, or shares, in the pool. The value of the gift, or the "fund" that the gift established, is the value of the fund's shares in the endowment pool. And the income attributable to this particular gift or fund is its pro rata share of the income of the endowment pool.[26] The result of the pooling is a single portfolio to be managed, serving many gifts or funds. An investment committee and a manager can concern themselves with the objectives and strategy for one pool instead of many.

Not all gifts can be placed in a pool, for some, by their own explicit terms, may require separate investment, and a single pool may fail to serve the differing purposes of all gifts. Two or three pools may be called for—perhaps a bond pool; a conservative, income-oriented common stock pool; and an aggressively invested common stock pool. A gift can be placed in the most appropriate pool or invested in more than one.

There are different approaches to the question of how much to spend from an endowment. The traditional rule has been to spend income yield (dividends, rents, interest, and so forth) but not capital appreciation, while recent years have seen a trend to a new rule (sanctioned by the Uniform Management of Institutional Funds Act) that permits spending a prudent portion of appreciation. Some institutions have placed some funds under the old rule and others under the new (see Chapter V). As a result, it is convenient to separate them into two pools—a "yield-only" pool and a "yield and appreciation" pool.

HOW LARGE SHOULD AN ENDOWMENT BE?

Many trustees will have a ready answer to this question: the larger the better. And there does not seem to be much point in defining an upper limit for endowments. But trustees do have a responsibility to estimate the minimum endowment necessary to fulfill their objectives for their institution.

A rather simple approach, one that is particularly appropriate to small institutions, calls for determining the endowment necessary to narrow the tuition gap to tolerable proportions. For example, if the tuition necessary to cover costs at a college is $3,000 per year when tuition at public institutions is $1,000, and if the trustees believe that their college can charge $1,200 more than public institutions and still succeed in attracting good students, then the college needs enough endowment to generate spending of $800 per student per year. If annual spending from the endowment is 5 percent of the endowment value, then the endowment needed is $16,000 per student. This at least establishes a "survival" endowment.

The experience of Yale University in 1973–74 may offer some insights into a thorough analysis of how much endowment an institution needs. In 1973, Richard C. Ferguson, then on the financial staff of Yale University, developed a Capital Requirements Model to estimate Yale's need for gift support. The model began with an estimate of 1972–73 income from a variety of sources, including tuition, dormitory, and meal charges. Each income item was placed in one of two categories: goods or services. (Some income items were divided between the two.) The purpose of the classification was to make possible projections of future income for each item, at a growth rate reflecting productivity increases (goods) or one not reflecting productivity (services). This procedure reflects the discussion earlier in this chapter with respect to inflation where productivity advances are being made (goods) and inflation in the areas of higher education where productivity appears to remain unchanged (services). Yale was then in a position to apply two different inflation rates in projecting income.

Next, the model incorporated an estimate of 1972–73 expenses, broken down by items, with the items once again allocated to either a goods or a services category. This made possible a projection of expenses, using the two expected rates of inflation.

The model was now ready to project the income and the expenses for future years for any estimate of the two inflation rates. The difference between income and expenses was treated as a gap to be filled with gifts plus spending from endowment.

Gifts for current use were projected to rise at the service inflation rate, and these were subtracted from the gap in order to arrive at the needed contribution from endowment. This year-by-year contribution was capitalized at the expected long-term rate of total return on the endowment to arrive at an estimate of the size of endowment Yale needed. This estimate depended, of course, on three critical forecasts: the rate of inflation in prices of goods, the rate of inflation for personal compensation, and the total return rate on the endowment. Using the model and making the forecasts, Yale determined a need for $161 million in new endowment to maintain the existing level of activities. And this amount became a part of the 1974–77 Campaign For Yale.

The model did not incorporate provisions for expanding or improving Yale's programs and facilities. A separate estimate was made for the endowment needed for these purposes. Further embellishments to the model are possible, but what is particularly useful about this model is that it could guide other institutions in developing their own general approach.

BUILDING ENDOWMENT: THE IMPORTANCE OF DEVELOPMENT

Building endowment through gifts may be as important as building it through investment performance. And in many cases, of course, gifts will be far more important than investment performance in turning an inadequate endowment fund into a satisfactory source of financial support.

Most colleges and universities, certainly the private ones, are engaged in some forms of fund raising. And most trustees have at least a general familiarity with development work, especially in their own institutions. But they may find useful a review of the kinds of development work that appear to be successful elsewhere.

Perhaps the most obvious college and university development is directed to alumni. Most institutions have an alumni fund that is expected to make an annual contribution to the institution's revenue. This contribution is generally directed to current spending rather than to the building of endowment. The success of an alumni fund appears to begin with a good deal of rather routine work, which assures that the institution keeps track of its alumni and keeps their interest. This means careful record keeping, the publication of an alumni magazine or at least newsletters, and regular solicitation. The operation of an alumni fund might be regarded as the basic development activity of an institution that produces fairly predictable revenues related to the development effort made.

A second alumni activity, less predictable and involving higher risks but also higher potential rewards, is the identification of special donors, usually by the institution's development staff, and a concentrated fund-raising effort directed to these individuals by the staff and perhaps by trustees and other volunteers. This approach, of course, can be carried beyond alumni to people of means, particularly in the institution's geographical area, and to parents of students and alumni. The reward from investment in this sort of development work will be slower than that from work on the alumni fund but quite significant.

A third alumni activity, also productive of slow rewards, is development of charitable remainder or life income gifts and bequests. A number of institutions assign one development officer to work exclusively on the attraction of life income gifts and bequests. The effectiveness of this officer will show up first in the attraction of life income gifts and perhaps much later in the form of bequests.

All of these development activities are important in soliciting alumni support, but a program that involves alumni in more than fund raising alone, one that includes such activities as carefully planned reunions and "alumni colleges" is critical.

Development work among corporations is also important. Obtaining gifts from major national corporations is quite difficult, except for an institution that has some special contact with these corporations or some outstanding activity that will attract their support. But an appeal to corporations in the institution's geographical area can be based upon the value of the institution to that area and, perhaps more specifically, upon the contribution the institution is making in providing well-educated employees for local commerce and industry.

Finally, we come to development work with foundations. Since the appeal to a foundation for financial support is likely to be based upon a very specific program or venture of the institution, faculty, department chairmen, and deans may play a particularly important role here. Indeed, in all fund raising, the development task is not operating in a vacuum; it needs the active cooperation and support of the entire institutional community. But in dealing with foundations, there is a special need for direct support by those responsible for the programs for which aid is sought. The principal contribution the development office can make is to keep abreast of foundations' policies and giving patterns, to spot opportunities for support, and to respond to requests from faculty and other academic people for help in seeking foundation support.

All of the activities described so far depend heavily upon a professional development staff within the institution. But individuals capable of giving substantial amounts are often best approached by a volunteer, another alumnus or alumna, or a trustee, for example, rather than by a professional development officer. The volunteers, however, can be effective only if backed up by a development staff to plan and organize the solicitation of individuals, to identify potential donors, and to thoroughly brief the volunteers.

Professional fund-raising counsel is often another source of support to the development staff, particularly in the planning of a major gift campaign, even in colleges and universities with large and experienced development staffs. The outsider brings more experience to a major campaign than any institutional staff can have. He can help plan budgets and timetables, identify resources needed in a campaign, and organize the campaign itself. In addition, he is sometimes better able than the inside staff to persuade trustees to make the necessary commitment of resources to a campaign.

Professional outside counsel can also be helpful on a regular basis. A monthly conference between the institution's chief development officer and the outside counsel can provide the institution with the experience of a person familiar with development work at many institutions, who can be helpful in reviewing the institution's program, identifying its achievements and failures, and helping to keep the program on course to its ultimate goal. This use of outside professional counsel may be especially beneficial in the training of the development officer. And the outside professional may be helpful in solving specific difficult problems by providing broader experience than is available within the institution. The development staff needs some direction whenever opportunities arise to influence the purpose of a gift. So it can be useful for the trustees of an institution, perhaps through a development committee, to maintain a continuous list of gift needs, reflecting their priorities for the college or university. Most institutions are now taking a closer look at unneeded gifts, especially those that entail some new expenses that must be met from the regular budget. This is particularly true with respect to buildings that have saddled many a college or university with staggering maintenance costs. And it may take some imagination to design endowment gifts that are as attractive to the donor as the "named" building. Still, gracious acceptance of a gift that means more to the donor than to the institution can be the beginning of a highly beneficial relationship.

Imagination is also called for in the form of gifts solicited. Traditionally, most gifts have come to colleges and universities as cash or marketable securities. But there are frequently opportunities for donors to give real estate, oil or gas interests, book royalties, or entire businesses. Knowing how to arrange a transfer of these properties (or being willing to find out how) and how to convert them into more manageable assets for the institution is a valuable quality in a development officer.

The development office itself should be regarded as a business operation and evaluated on the basis of its productivity, since reducing the resources of a development effort that is making good use of those resources does nothing for the financial health of an institution. Some institutions have begun to charge the cost of development activities against capital gift campaigns, applying only the net gift to specific or general purposes. It may also be appropriate to charge current gifts with development expenses. This could help to identify the productivity of development and to charge its costs against the activities directly benefited by gifts. But there are some dangers here. First, a donor who wishes to benefit a particular activity of the institution may quickly lose enthusiasm when confronted with an "overhead" charge. And second, there is great value in a united institutional development effort, with all members of the institution willing to help raise funds for any part of it. This cooperative effort may be jeopardized by charging development costs among the direct beneficiaries of gifts.

It is probably well worthwhile for any institution that anticipates a more or less permanent life to have at least one able development officer who can not only supervise the alumni activity but can also give some thought to the solicitation of nonalumni individuals.

Cooperation from all parts of the institution is clearly valuable to a development staff. It can be particularly important that development people understand the operations of the endowment fund and have confidence in its management and in the endowment-spending policy the trustees have established. Communicating this understanding and confidence can be critical in soliciting contributions to endowment and in supporting current operations.

In trying to assess the development effort at their own institution, trustees may find it useful to make some comparisons with other institutions. *Voluntary Support of Education*, which gives some aggregate statistics and provides details for a substantial number of colleges and universities, all identified by name, may be helpful.[27] By looking through the detailed statistics, one can get some idea of what is possible through development and some idea of what essentially similar institutions have been able to accomplish. For example, the ratio of the number of alumni donors to the number of alumni solicited will give some indication of the effectiveness of the development activity, as will the average size of the alumni gift. One has to consider these statistics as a set. It may be misleading to single out one and attempt to use it alone to evaluate a development effort. For example, one approach to alumni may lead to a very high proportion of donors but a low average gift, while another, more sharply focused, may produce fewer responses but larger gifts.

Comparisons of gift receipts through bequests, annuities, and life income contracts will help to indicate whether the institution is missing some opportunities. Comparisons of support from foundations are also useful. Relatively small support from foundations may be an indication that an institution does not have the programs and the academic quality necessary to attract this support, or it may suggest that insufficient effort has been made.

An in erested trustee can make a variety of other statistical comparisons. And one of these, going beyond the question of the effectiveness of the development effort, concerns the relative proportion of gifts for annual operating support and gifts for capital purposes. Faced with current needs for funds, as virtually all institutions are, a college or university may be tempted to put the major part of its efforts into raising funds to meet annual operating expenses. A dollar added this year to endowment may seem to contribute very little to meeting next year's budget. But there are high risks involved in a heavy dependence on current gifts, which can lead to taking on permanent expense obligations in the expectation that these gifts will continue. A good many institutions take a significant portion of the unrestricted gifts for current use and add it to endowment rather than spend it.

GOVERNMENT SUPPORT FOR ENDOWMENT

Direct public support for private colleges and universities has taken at least three forms:

1. Programs to subsidize needy students and to provide subsidized or guaranteed loan funds have enabled more students to meet the tuition charges of private institutions.
2. Public grants to underwrite specific programs, particularly research activities, or private institutions have made these programs possible.
3. Subsidies or guarantees to facilitate institutional borrowing for the construction of buildings have made building possible.

Unfortunately, all three forms of support pose serious risks. Institutions that have accepted public support and come to depend upon it have discovered the disastrous consequences of cutbacks either because of governmental economy or changes in priorities. The risks have been especially high when the support, particularly for programs and for buildings, has led institutions into long-run commitments that might not otherwise have been undertaken.

Acceptance of government support also entails a sacrifice of independence. The United States is the only nation that still has truly independent private institutions of higher education. In the United Kingdom and in Canada, institutions that were at one time financially and academically independent have gradually come under public control. Canadian "private" universities are fast yielding the last remnants of autonomy.[28]

The least threatening form of public support to emerge so far is
probably direct student aid, sometimes through the form of tuition
vouchers, which can be used at private as well as public institutions,
and sometimes through guaranteed and subsidized student loans.
Even these programs, of course, pose the possibility of cutback or
withdrawal.

Indirect government aid for building endowment comes chiefly
from the deductibility of gifts to colleges and universities for tax purposes. Some studies on the importance of the deductibility of these
gifts are underway as part of the work of the Commission on Private
Philanthropy and Public Needs (the Filer Commission). They may
suggest what the cost to higher education would be of further efforts
to curtail deductions in the name of tax reform.

A NEW APPROACH TO ENDOWMENT BUILDING:
THE COLLEGE ENDOWMENT FUNDING PLAN

Building endowment, with or without government aid, is a task
that calls for imagination and ingenuity. A particularly interesting
idea has come recently from Dr. F. D. Patterson, chairman of the
Moton Memorial Institute, a founder of the United Negro College
Fund, and a former president of Tuskegee Institute. Faced with the
dilemma of financial crisis without government aid and the high risks
that go with that aid, Dr. Patterson has proposed the College Endowment Funding Plan. His starting point is the proven success of "challenge" grants, which are based on the condition that an institution
raise matching funds. There are not enough wealthy donors to provide all the needed challenges, and Dr. Patterson has proposed low-
cost loans as a substitute. The loans would come either from private
lenders (probably corporations) willing to accept a below-market rate
of interest or from a federal or state agency able to borrow at less than
corporate rates. The loans would be made available to match gifts in
some appropriate ratio of loan to gift, just as challenge gifts are, and
the loan funds would combine with the gift funds to build endowment. For example, the plan might permit a college that has raised
$100,000 in gifts to borrow up to $300,000 and invest the $400,000
total. Out of the income from this investment the college would amortize the loan and draw some revenue for current use. Once the loan

had been repaid, the college would have $400,000 of unencumbered endowment.

Research on the plan, coordinated by The Common Fund, has established the conditions under which it is economically viable. A small pilot project relying on a group of private lenders has been in the development stage since early 1975.

II/*Objectives and Management for the Endowment*

There is plenty of room for disagreement as to the best form of organization for the handling of endowment funds. And because what is best for one institution is not necessarily best for another, it is difficult to offer a universal prescription. But it is clear that the disappointing investment results of many endowments are due to poor organization, unclear lines of responsibility, and inept establishment or monitoring of objectives.[1] Accumulated experience in the field suggests useful options for improving the results of the management process and practical methods that trustees can employ to avoid repeating the mistakes of others.

THE ROLES OF THE BOARD OF TRUSTEES
AND THE INVESTMENT COMMITTEE

The board of trustees is responsible for the management and use of the endowment. But part of the management function has to be delegated, at least to a committee of the board and probably even further—to a professional manager. This leads to two questions: How much of the management responsibility should be retained by the full board,[2] and how is this responsibility to be put in its proper perspective as part of the whole process of overseeing the affairs of the institution.

In every institution, the board must be in a position to hold accountable those to whom responsibility is delegated. If the determination of investment objectives, for example, is left to an investment committee, then there must be a system of reporting and reviewing that not only permits but requires the full board to consider and approve or disapprove the objectives proposed by the committee.

49

Even further, there should be a means of evaluating and, if necessary, replacing the committee or some of its members.

It is not easy for members of a board of trustees to sit in judgment of one another, and it is particularly difficult to displace gracefully a member who has given long service and who may well have done much for the institution outside his or her committee work. A board that is willing to plan for problems—such as domination of an investment committee by a strong chairman—before they arise may be able to work out some systematic devices that will help to avoid awkward situations. For example, automatic rotation of committee memberships can be helpful; some institutions permit a trustee to serve up to two five-year terms on a committee, followed by a year off the committee before reappointment. This makes it relatively easy to bring in new viewpoints and avoid long-term dominance by an individual but does not seriously hamper long-term contribution by able trustees. Continuity can also be preserved by staggering terms, so that one member of the investment committee, for example, is replaced each year.

Since the investment objectives are part of the overall financial policy for an institution, it may seem appropriate for the full board to establish the policy and the objectives. But it is probably more appropriate for an investment committee to put together a set of investment objectives and to present them to the full board as part of a financial policy than for the full board to initiate the process. In this case, the board may have to press the committee rather strongly for a set of objectives spelled out in such a way that it is possible to evaluate them before approval and possible to tell as time goes on whether the investment committee is actually following these objectives. To draw up objectives of this sort is an extraordinarily difficult task, entailing assessment of the relative proportions of bonds, stocks, and cash; the quality level of stocks; diversification and growth objectives; the emphasis on growth and cyclical stocks; the quality and maturity of bonds; whether there is to be market timing, and if so, who will make the timing decision; and how and when the management of the fund is to be evaluated against the objectives.

Selection, or at least approval of the selection, of a professional investment manager is sometimes seen as a function of the board, rather than of an investment committee. Review of the investment performance of the manager is another responsibility that might fall to either the board or the committee. A review by the full board of the work of the investment committee can hardly avoid a careful consideration of investment performance, but whether the board or the committee has the direct responsibility for the manager's performance may depend upon the preferences of a particular board.

There seems to be almost unanimous agreement that the board should stay away from consideration of individual purchases or sales of securities. This is what professional managers are hired to do. There may be exceptions, as when a manager wishes to dispose of a security and there is a likelihood that the disposition will alienate an important supporter of the institution, so that more than an investment decision is involved. But one might expect that most of these cases could be resolved by the investment committee, without reference to the board.

It is harder to decide whether the board, rather than the investment committee, should establish an approved ratio of stock and bond holdings. There is widespread agreement that this decision is the single most important aspect of setting an investment policy.

The board must face the question of what reports or other information are necessary for the monitoring of investment objectives. The conclusion of the Ford Foundation sponsored study, *Managing Educational Endowments*, more commonly called the Barker Report, was this:

> Measurement is one of the essential ingredients in achieving first-class results. If one does not know whether the record is good or bad, why try to improve it? We urge that all trustees insist on (a) regular measurement of the investment results for their institution; (b) regular comparison to those of other colleges and mutual funds; and (c) cold-blooded analysis of whether the performance is good enough. Except in the case of obvious incompetence, we think a final judgment about the manager should be withheld for as long as three years to allow for short-term price fluctuations that sometimes obscure for a considerable period of time the merit of an excellent long-term investment policy. We believe that three years should normally be long enough to permit such merit to be reflected in the investment results.[3]

The rate of appreciation or depreciation in market value and the income yield, which together make up the total return on the endowment, are the "investment results" referred to here. There are some who will argue that the criteria suggested by the Barker Report are not what the trustees should use to monitor either the investment committee or the manager. The trustees should be concerned with how well the set of investment objectives is being met; and unless the objectives simply call for maximum total return, the total return comparisons will not meet the trustees' needs. The Barker Report, in fact, urged that maximum total return, in the long run, should be the primary objective of endowment fund management. And the report avoided explicit consideration of risk as an objective. One can at least argue that, if the institution has adopted an investment policy that does specify an appropriate risk level, comparisons should be made to funds with similar levels of risk. And it seems equally appropriate to ask for evidence that the endowment fund is actually being managed at the chosen risk level, whatever its total return has been.

Some would brush aside completely the comparisons suggested in the Barker Report, on the grounds that each institution has a set of unique objectives and no other fund is truly comparable. There is some reason to suspect that this attitude rests more on a wish to avoid embarrassing comparisons than on anything else.

In any case, it may be preferable to rely on a full-market cycle, rather than on an arbitrary three years or any other fixed time period, in making an evaluation. This is particularly important if total return comparisons are being made among funds.

The board must have the means of determining how well its investment objectives are being met and whether other funds are doing better or worse at meeting similar objectives. Five or six years ago, very few boards of trustees had statements of investment policy precise enough to permit a judgment as to whether the policy was being followed or even knew the true investment performance of their endowments, let alone how that performance compared with others.

At many institutions, the spending policy is regarded as quite separate from the investment policy. And indeed the spending policy may be developed by a finance committee of the board, while the investment objectives are proposed by the investment committee. As far as the full board is concerned, the spending and investment policies need not be combined in a single statement of objectives, but it is crucial that they be consistent (and consistent with fund-raising objectives, as well).

The board must determine the role that the endowment is to play in providing financial support. The balance between current spending and growth to support future spending is probably the most important part of the endowment fund policy and should certainly be considered carefully by the full board.

In recent years, boards of trustees have begun to concern themselves with a further policy issue: the social responsibilities of the investor. The issue was presented most dramatically a few years ago when students and faculty on some campuses demanded that their institutions dispose of stockholdings in corporations whose products, labor practices, or other policies were seen as undesirable. At some of the institutions, trustees responded by creating a mechanism to deal with social responsibilities. At others, there was resistance to any interference with traditional investment practices.

Today, there is less controversy based on strong emotional feelings, but a decision is still called for. At the least, a board of trustees must decide how proxies are to be voted, bearing in mind that many corporate proxies today call for votes on matters raised by shareholders rather than by management. Some boards will want assurance that their institution does not own securities of corporations whose behavior is inconsistent with the standards and philosophy of their institution, although it is at best extraordinarily difficult to clearly identify those standards and that philosophy and compare corporate behavior against them. Other boards will want affirmative action taken to try to change undesirable corporate behavior.

Many institutions have set up a committee of students, faculty, and alumni (sometimes of trustees, as well) to advise the investment committee on the voting of proxies, the avoidance or disposition of investments in socially unattractive corporations, and the possible communication with corporate managements to urge changes in behavior.[4]

Most institutions have an investment committee made up of the trustees, which is charged solely with supervision of the institution's investments. In a few institutions, however, a finance committee is charged with broad responsibility for all aspects of the institution's finances, including investments and the budget. For institutions with substantial endowments, there seems to be a preference for an investment committee separate from the finance committee (or perhaps for a subcommittee of the finance committee).[5]

About all that the typical full board of trustees has demanded of its investment committee is a report from the committee at the regular board meetings. And until recent years these reports rarely provided a basis for judging the quality either of the committee's work or of the work of the professional manager. Only quite extraordinary developments, such as a switch from the traditional yield-only spending rule to a rule permitting the spending of some appreciation (see Chapter V), seem to have called for any action on the part of the full board.

The membership of investment committees has tended to be fairly large, with many consisting of 8 to 12 members, who are usually drawn from the trustees whose principal occupations were in the fields of commercial banking, stock brokerage, investment banking, and law.[6]

There are widely varying opinions as to the kind of trustees who should be included on an investment committee. An ignorance of the investment world and of matters financial may seem an obvious handicap. Yet too much expertise can result in unproductive debates within the committee and some loss of perspective on the appropriate role of the investment committee. Probably any intelligent trustee, with a willingness to learn, is an appropriate candidate for an investment committee. Specific expertise is relevant if the committee itself engages in direct day-to-day management of the endowment portfolio. But it is precisely this committee activity, one that most committees delegate to a professional, full-time manager, that may be the source of ineffective management.

Commercial bankers, as a group, have a poor reputation as members of investment committees. In part, this is because other trustees expect too much in the way of investment expertise: the work of a commercial banker may have little to do with investments. Unfortunately, at some institutions, bankers have been happy to accept the full confidence of their fellow committee members, to the extent of dominating the committee's decision making. At other institutions, commercial bankers on the committee have made a practice of referring all recommendations to their bank trust departments and then arguing with the fund manager on the basis of the trust department opinions. Lawyers have a mixed reputation. Some have won great respect from fellow committee members, while others have caused frustration with their constantly "legalistic" attitudes. Professional investment managers suggest that a successful businessman is a prime candidate for the committee, on the grounds that he is likely to have learned to delegate management and will not constantly second-guess the manager. Another suggestion is a professional investment manager, one who has disqualified himself from ever managing the institution's endowment, so that he cannot be seen as competing for the position.

Although it might seem reasonable to choose the membership of an investment committee to reflect a wide range of investment attitudes, particularly of willingness to take risks, such a wide range might present a professional manager with problems. His recommendations must be aimed at the middle of the range, and he knows there will be some who will argue that he is too aggressive, while others will complain that he is too conservative. And if it is uncertain which members will attend a meeting, the manager has a particularly

difficult time planning his recommendations. The manager will probably prefer an agreed-upon philosophy of the committee or even
domination of the committee by an individual whose attitudes are
predictable.

INVESTMENT POLICY

There is rather general agreement that the chief role of the investment committee is to formulate an investment policy, which almost certainly should be subject to review and approval by the full
board. The policy must be set in the context of an overall financial
plan, and this, in turn, must be consistent with the overall objectives of
the institution. There are many possible methods of deducing an
investment policy, and no one can prescribe a procedure that will
serve all institutions well. But here is a specific example: A five- to
ten-year financial plan is critical as a starting point. Some will object
that a projection ten years into the future is impossible, but even a
rough projection with all its unknowns is infinitely better than none at
all, and a growing practice is a fairly detailed five-year budget followed by a rough budget for years six to ten.

Such a projected financial plan may treat endowment revenue as
a balancing figure, subtracting other anticipated revenues from total
expected spending. If the gap left cannot be filled by the endowment,
then the projections must be revised—some expenditures cut, for
example, or greater fund-raising commitments undertaken—until
the target for the endowment contribution appears reasonable.

Once the investment committee has established a target for
spending from endowment over a period of several years (for example, a spending level of 4 percent of the value of the endowment, with
the endowment growing at 7 percent a year), it should consult with
those who manage the endowment assets on a day-to-day basis—the
professional managers—to decide on what kind of investment
strategy, if any, can reasonably produce the necessary rate of return.
The answer may well be that an 11 percent rate of return is a reasonable long-run target only if the institution is willing to take a great deal
of investment risk, more than the investment committee is prepared
to recommend. In this case, the investment committee can only return
to the finance committee to call for another revision in the expenditure plans or in the plans for other revenue sources.

The ultimate product from adapting plans and expectations is a
set of projected expenditures and revenues, an expected total-return

rate for the endowment, and a description of the degree of risk that accompanies this return expectation. The overall plan generated by the finance and investment committees will be internally consistent and consistent with the trustee's general strategy for the institution, for the present and for future years. The full board will finally review a complete financial plan, any part of which might be altered but not without corresponding alteration to other parts.

The investment policy should be expressed in at least two dimensions: the expected rate of return and the corresponding level of risk. But a committee or a board can go farther and describe the kinds of investments contemplated to meet these objectives: the relative proportions of bonds and stocks; the kinds of bonds—in terms of quality ratings, maturities, and types; and the kinds of stocks—in terms of quality, emphasis on growth, and so forth. The description will help to provide assurance that the return and risk objectives can probably be achieved and put the level of risk in comprehensible terms.

RISK AS AN OBJECTIVE

No one should have much difficulty comprehending what is meant by a target rate of return of 11 percent a year. It is a very different matter to describe a level of risk-taking that is generally comprehensible and means the same thing to all trustees. Chapter III deals with investment performance and with performance measures, including risk measures.

One approach to determining the potential for loss in a portfolio is to consult with the professional manager. There are reasons for doubting whether this is a useful method. Intuitive feelings about the likelihood of loss on a portfolio have proved disastrously unreliable in recent years, and, of course, a professional manager almost has to be optimistic. To admit that his portfolio offers greater risk of loss than his competitors are claiming for their portfolios may mean a loss of clients. And finally, an investment committee has no way to determine whether the portfolio *is* actually as risky as the manager says it is.

A significant element of risk in a diversified stock portfolio is market-related—stock portfolios rise in value when the stock market rises and fall when the market falls. This risk element is usually referred to as "volatility" and applies to bond portfolios as well, for bond prices rise when interest rates decline and fall when interest rates rise. For some institutions, the market value of a bond portfolio may be of little concern, since bonds can be held to maturity; but for institutions that base spending on market value, volatility in bonds is important.

The performance of the market is beyond the control of the manager. What is largely within his control is the relationship of his portfolio to the market. He can assemble either a portfolio of stocks that is very sensitive to the market and a portfolio of bonds that is very sensitive to interest rates or portfolios that are not so sensitive. So the volatility measure is a measure of something that is under the manager's control and that can be used to monitor his use of that control.

The calendar years 1973–74 were an extraordinarily bad period for stocks generally. The Standard & Poor's Composite Index (the "500" Index), which is a broadly based stock index, achieved a total return (depreciation offset by income) of −36.7 percent in those years, or −20.5 percent a year. Interest rates rose during the period, and the Salomon Brothers Long-Term High-Grade Corporate Bond Index showed a total return (again depreciation offset by income) of −1.9 percent for the two years, or −1 percent a year.

Taking 1973–74 as an extreme case of poor market performance, an investment committee could determine what kind of portfolio would have led to tolerable losses in that year and hence represents a tolerable volatility level. Suppose that 70 percent of the total endowment portfolio is invested in common stocks, and the common stock component of the portfolio is designed to mirror the performance of the stock market as a whole. And suppose that the remaining 30 percent of the endowment is invested in long-term corporate bonds reflecting the performance of the Salomon Brothers Index.

$$70\% \times -36.7\% + 30\% \times -1.9\% = -26.3\%.$$

Then the total portfolio would probably produce a total return of −26.3 percent for the period, or −14.2 percent a year. It is worth remembering that bonds are volatile too and can lead to market-value losses, although they are generally a good deal smaller than stock market losses.

If the investment committee is prepared to tolerate risk of an even greater loss in another period like 1973–74 (in the hope of raising the total-return expectation), it could adjust the portfolio strategy to allow for more stocks, a more volatile stock portfolio, or perhaps a greater exposure to risk in the bond portfolio. And if the committee feels a potential loss of 26 percent in a period like 1973–74 is intolerable, it can shift the strategy to call for more or safer bonds (or cash) or less volatile stocks.

PORTFOLIO COMPOSITION

The allocation of the portfolio among stocks and bonds (and short-term investments) is clearly a critical element in an investment policy, and setting this ratio may appear to involve only a consideration of the volatility exposure that is appropriate for the institution. Changes in the ratio then would follow only from changes in the institution's tolerance for volatility. But professional managers almost all argue that the ratio should also change with expectations as to the performance of the market. If a manager can forecast securities markets, shifting among cash, stocks, and bonds should result in a portfolio that consistently does better than either market and one that involves less volatility than either market (see Chapter III). While this result is theoretically attractive, there is little evidence that professional managers actually achieve it.[7] An important policy question then is whether the allocation of assets among cash, bonds, and stocks should be solely a function of long-run rate of return targets and volatility tolerance, which would probably mean very few changes in the proportions, or whether they should be altered to reflect short-run expectations and therefore attempt to outperform the market.

A significant advantage of the first policy is the reduced likelihood of a committee floundering back and forth among cash, bonds, and stocks as expectations change and markets move rapidly up and down. At more than one institution, such floundering has turned to near panic, and some institutions switched from stocks to bonds at the bottom of the stock market in 1974. Adherence to a policy of fixed allocations, coupled with an understanding of what is likely to happen in different markets, can enable an investment committee to weather these storms successfully.

Specifying the allocation of assets among stocks, bonds, and short-term investments is a useful but rather crude way to establish a volatility level. A more precise specification would be helpful, and I will start with the bonds.

The purpose of including bonds in a portfolio is to reduce risk—stocks are almost certainly more profitable in the long run—or perhaps to increase current income yield. It is possible to reduce the risk in an all-stock portfolio by shifting to the safest stocks, but using bonds is more efficient. Not only are bonds generally much more stable than stocks, but they offer a diversification—the bond market is only moderately correlated with the stock market.

As a general rule, not only do long-term bonds offer a higher expected rate of return than short-term bonds, but they also involve greater risk of price decline. A bond manager can present the investment committee with the approximate relationship between expected return and volatility and between maturity and volatility; and the committee can make its choice, specifying the acceptable average maturity. The committee will also have to decide whether to authorize the manager to shift the average maturity on the basis of his interest rate forecasts.

Quality ratings also have a bearing on expected rate of return and risk. The risk, a credit risk rather than a market risk, is much harder to measure, partly because we have little recent history of bond defaults. But the committee will have to strike a compromise here also, between risk and return.

Marketability and diversification are a little harder to deal with in precise terms. An investment committee should give some thought to the institution's need for marketability before insisting that securities be readily marketable. The need may actually be small, unless there is an expectation that the portfolio will be shifted frequently among different assets.

Stocks present a more difficult problem because there is less general agreement on classification criteria. Some academic research has been aimed at identifying appropriate classes of common stock— classes useful for specifying the allocation of a stock portfolio. James Farrell has discussed this material in two articles; in one he identifies growth, cyclical, stable, and oil stocks as homogeneous classes.[8] Démarche Associates of Kansas City, Missouri, has devised a classification system that appears to produce groups of stocks that are genuinely homogeneous in terms of a variety of commonly accepted characteristics, like growth and quality, and in terms of performance under different market conditions. And the differences among the Démarche groups seem consistent and logical. Using this kind of classification, an investment committee can break down its common stock allocation by groups, with some confidence that the end result will fit the overall return and risk target. Once again, the committee will have to decide how much latitude a manager should have in shifting allocations among categories of stocks.

The investment committee needs professional advice on risk and return characteristics of securities when setting investment objectives. Since the investment manager has a personal stake in the match between his aptitudes and the committee's objectives, it may be best not to rely on him until the investment committee has a clear idea of its objectives. But once the objectives are set, a discussion with the manager should establish just what he is expected to do.

Specifying risk level in terms of exposure to loss, then in terms of allocation of assets among stocks, bonds, and money market instruments, and finally in terms of categories of these major classifications can provide a standard that is both comprehensible and useful in monitoring performance. The graph in Figure 2-1 can be useful in tracking the performance of an entire portfolio against a set of investment objectives.

The graph shows the monthly total return rate for The Common Fund, month-by-month from July 1974 through June 1975, plotted against the total return for the Standard & Poor's Composite Index. The points plotted are labeled by month (275 indicates February 1975), and a straight line has been fitted through the points to de-

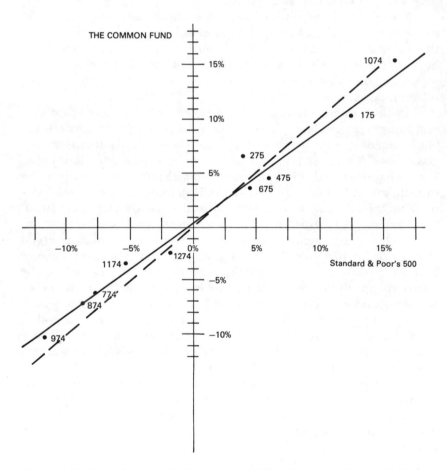

Figure 2-1. Total Return Performance of The Common Fund, 12 Months Ending June 1975, Plotted against the Total Return on the Standard & Poor's 500 Index

scribe the general relationship between The Common Fund's performance and the performance of the stock market. The slope of this line is .909, a little less than 1. (A dashed line with a slope of 1 has been drawn in for comparison.)

Since the points plotted lie very close to the fitted line, this means that the relationship of fund to market was very stable during this period. (The correlation coefficient, which measures the closeness of fit, is .99; for a perfect fit, the correlation would be 1.0.)

The graph shows the general relationship between the fund and the market; it shows how consistent the relationship was; it reveals, as each month is plotted, whether there has been a significant deviation; and it shows whether the managers have succeeded in selecting better-than-average securities. Finally, and this is a far more trivial function, the graph can serve to channel alarm over declining values in a year like 1974 into a careful consideration of whether the fund is being properly managed, given a market over which neither trustees nor manager has any control.

There is no way of accurately predicting just what the market is capable of producing in performance results, so the results of a risk level specified in terms of market relationships cannot be accurately predicted. And even for a well-diversified portfolio, the relationships are never exactly what is called for in the statement of investment objectives. There are still many trustees and many professional managers who feel uneasy with these quantitative aspects of risk and suggest, with some justification, that the measurements conceal deficiencies in reliability under a mask of numerical precision.

But more and more experienced professionals are turning to these measures because no other approach to risk description appears to offer even a reasonable chance of precision and satisfactory monitoring of performance. The investment committee that is content to set objectives in terms of "acceptable risk level" will probably never know just what each trustee had in mind when the policy was approved, will probably not know just what the professional manager understood by the terms, and will almost certainly be unable to determine whether the manager has followed the statement of objectives.

SETTING THE RISK LEVEL

Having established the terms in which objectives are to be stated and, in particular, the terms in which the risk level is to be described, the committee must reach a conclusion as to what that level should be. This is, at best, a complex business and involves a consideration of the sources of financial risk within the institution itself as a guide to the amount of investment risk that is acceptable in the endowment fund.

The relative importance of the endowment in furnishing financial support to the institution must be considered. If this support is trivial, if it is, for example, on the order of 1 or 2 percent of the budget, then even substantial losses suffered by the endowment fund will not have a great impact on the institution's overall financial position. It may well be that a strategy involving quite high investment risks, in the expectation of achieving substantial growth in the endowment fund, will be justified.[9] On the other hand, if the endowment is contributing a substantial part of the institutional budget, then the permissible risk level in the fund itself will be a good deal lower.

The particular sources of the institution's revenue, as well as expenses, will involve their own risks. A heavy dependence upon government support for research activities, and perhaps indirectly for educational activities, presents risks that are all too familiar to the institutions whose government support has been drastically reduced in recent years. Even a heavy dependence upon gifts for current use presents risks through possible disenchantment on the part of the donors. Expenses, too, are a source of financial risk; for example, unanticipated inflation is by now a familiar problem to most institutions.

Revenue from endowment can provide diversification and reduce overall risk. And the risk level of the endowment itself can be adjusted to the particular circumstances of the institution.

In short, what really underlies a good endowment policy is a consideration of the probable interplay of a variety of sources of revenue and causes of expenditure, each with its own degree of uncertainty and all somewhat related. The mind of the most astute analyst may boggle at the prospect of intuitively combining all of these uncertainties and relationships in order to come up with a satisfactory overall financial policy and finally a good endowment policy. Simulation techniques have been devised to deal with this sort of problem, but only a few colleges and universities (Yale and Stanford[10] among them) have made much use of them for financial planning.[11]

PORTFOLIO MANAGEMENT

At some institutions, day-to-day decisions regarding the purchase and sale of portfolio securities or whatever other assets may be held by the endowment fund are still made by the investment committee. The Harris Associates Survey in 1971 indicated that the investment committees made these decisions at over 20 percent of the 214 colleges and universities surveyed, although most of them made use of a professional adviser.[12]

Interviews at 31 universities in 1968 revealed considerable dissatisfaction with portfolio decision making by the Committee.[13] Many investment committees found it difficult and all found it time-consuming to reach even simple decisions on the purchase and sale of securities, particularly when the committee included several representatives of the financial community who held conflicting views as to appropriate specific investments. Most investment committees seemed to operate by consensus, so that one member was generally able to block any particular transaction. Few investment committees met frequently enough to deal with changing conditions. The Harris Associates Survey supports this conclusion,[14] and the Barker Report states that investment committee involvement in these decisions "has been a basic cause of the relatively poor performance of so many . . . endowments."[15] Hired professional advisers may be helpful, but some of these advisers feel considerable frustration when their advice is ignored. At the same time, some institutions have quite substantial endowment funds for which the portfolio decisions are made by the investment committee, with the advice of a hired professional adviser, and neither the investment committee nor the full board of trustees have indicated any dissatisfaction with this procedure.[16] Trustees, of course, have difficulty openly finding fault with the work of fellow trustees. This is a factor that should be considered in determining who should carry out a task for which evaluation is important. As one experienced financial officer puts it: "How can the investment committee criticize performance when each member has his turnip in the pie?"

At most institutions, the day-to-day management of the endowment—the portfolio decision-making—is delegated to a full-time professional manager, either an employee of the institution—an "inside" manager—or an independent professional organization—an "outside" manager.[17]

A majority of institutions employ a portfolio manager outside the institution itself.[18] For institutions with very small endowment funds, this is likely to take the form of investment in The Common Fund.[19] At institutions with larger endowments, portfolio management is entrusted to a bank trust department, investment counseling firm, broker, investment banker, insurance company, or mutual fund management company that offers portfolio management service. A few universities have set up their own investment management staffs. The Harvard and Yale examples are discussed briefly below.

Professional managers enjoy varying degrees of autonomy; the range runs from full discretion through discretion subject to guidelines and discretion limited to an approved list to a requirement that the investment committee approve all portfolio transactions in advance.[20]

LEGAL ASPECTS OF DELEGATION

In general, over the years the responsibility for direct management of the endowment portfolio has gradually shifted from the board of trustees to an investment committee and on to a professional manager. The Barker Report suggested that this process had been slowed by the reluctance on the part of college and university trustees to delegate what they see as their personal responsibility for the management of the institution's funds.

In 1969, William L. Cary and Craig B. Bright explored the state of the law with respect to the delegation of investment responsibilities by trustees of educational institutions.[21] They had little difficulty in ascertaining the legal propriety of delegating investment functions to officials of the educational institution itself, and they argued that a charitable corporation also *should* be free to delegate the power to buy and sell securities for an endowment to *outside* investment counsel, provided that the investment counsel furnished prompt reports and that the delegation arrangement could be terminated at any time. They suggested that the use of an approved list of securities would make this practice legally more defensible and suggested other limitations within which such outside counsel might have to work.

Five years later Cary and Bright reaffirmed their conclusion with respect to delegation within the institution and presented the results of a more thorough investigation of external delegation.[22] By this time 13 states had adopted the Uniform Management of Institutional Funds Act, authorizing delegation of investment management in the following terms:

> SECTION 5. [*Delegation of Investment Management.*] Except as otherwise provided by the applicable gift instrument or by applicable law relating to governmental institutions of funds, the governing board may (1) delegate to its committees, officers or employees of the institution or the fund, or agents, including investment counsel, the authority to act in place of the board in investment and reinvestment of institutional funds, (2) contract with independent investment advisors, investment counsel or managers, banks, or trust companies, so to act, and (3) authorize

the payment of compensation for investment advisory or management services.

Some other states have other legislation permitting outside delegation. For example, New York and Pennsylvania permit nonprofit corporations to transfer endowment funds to a bank or trust company in the state. California has a similar statute, and Louisiana permits the deposit of endowment funds with the state treasurer, for investment in bonds of Louisiana or the United States.[23]

Apart from these statutes, Cary and Bright found little direct, authoritative data on the extent to which the management of charitable endowment funds may be delegated to an outside manager. The legal objections to delegation are a part of the law of trusts, and even this law permits a trustee to discharge some of his duties through an agent. But Cary and Bright argued that corporate law, rather than trust law, should serve as the guide to delegation by an educational institution, since as a matter of corporate law, the delegation of full investment management would not be objectionable. Even so, Cary and Bright maintained that the delegation should be made terminable at will or on relatively short notice.[24]

SELECTION OF A MANAGER

A great deal of statistical analysis of the results achieved by different portfolio managers suggests that it is very difficult to identify portfolio managers who can deliver truly superior investment performance, and those who can be identified are likely to produce only a modestly superior performance. This does not mean that an investment manager can be chosen just as well by random selection as through careful screening. But it does mean that an intensive search for the best performing manager may be less useful than many investment committees, particularly those that sought out high-performance managers in the late 1960s, have assumed.

Perhaps the best way to picture the management selection process is in terms of achieving a "fit" with the endowment's investment objectives. It is critical that the manager find the objectives congenial in terms of the way in which they are specified, the specific return and risk targets, and the degree of discretion available to him. It is equally critical that the capabilities of the manager match these requirements. The classification system for equities that I discussed earlier, developed by Démarche Associates, is accompanied by a system for matching managers' abilities to an institution's choices of asset allocations and for subsequently evaluating the managers in terms of performance of each asset category, testing the consistency between expectations and accomplishment, forecasting, and stock selection ability.[25]

There has been a tendency in the past to choose a manager simply on the strength of his apparent ability to achieve high rates of return. Recent years have seen a move to a more sensible emphasis on a close match between the particular objectives of an institution and the particular abilities, interests, and motivations of a manager.

John F. Meck, the president of the board of trustees of The Common Fund, has described the process by which portfolio managers were chosen for the fund in 1969 and 1970.[26] The procedure reflects a good deal of care and thought and was probably about as thorough a process as any institution had used up to that date to select managers for an endowment fund (Despite this, the trustees found it necessary to replace one of the two original managers after three years.)

The Common Fund Board of Trustees set up a selection committee composed of 5 of its 12 members. The committee in turn employed two consultants who had some experience in the process of selecting portfolio managers. In the fall of 1969, the committee and the consultants prepared a list of over two hundred possible managers and, after lengthy discussion, reduced this list to 50 candidates who represented a broad geographical area and included investment counseling firms, banks, and brokerage firms. To achieve diversification in management styles, the board then decided to retain more than one manager.

All 50 candidates were invited to appear for an interview, and 43 responded. By January 1970, the two consultants had interviewed all 43. As the screening process went on, the consultants and the selection committee developed six criteria by which to make a final judgment. One criterion was a workload that would permit the organization to devote adequate resources to The Common Fund. A second criterion concerned the organization's investment decision-making process—its capacity for economic forecasting, securities research, trading and accounting, and good internal communications. A third criterion was orientation—toward tax-free pension or endowment funds rather than taxable accounts of corporations or individuals. There was also concern for the importance the organization apparently attached to The Common Fund account, and therefore the kind of talent that would be assigned to it, and that the investment

tives being pursued by the managers within an organization should be consistent with the objectives of The Common Fund itself.

A fourth criterion was the experience and reputation of individual managers within an organization and the apparent ability of the people within that organization to work together. A fifth criterion was life cycle, which had to do with whether the organization appeared to be in a dynamic growth period of its life, in a period of stable maturity, or in a period of decline. A sixth criterion was past performance that could be said to truly represent the capabilities of an organization. Much depended upon the time period to which the performance records applied and to the choice of accounts from which the records were drawn. Moreover, many organizations had a great deal of personnel turnover; their performance records therefore were likely to reflect the work of individuals who had moved on. Hence the selection committee and the consultants concluded that they should look for consistency in performance—for an apparently sensible investment decision-making process that worked well in practice in a variety of investment environments.

The consultants tabulated the fees charged by each of the organizations interviewed, but fee levels never became an important issue in the selection process.

The consultants brought to the selection committee their detailed analysis of the 43 applicants, including a rating of each of the applicants on the basis of the six criteria discussed above. The selection committee then invited 15 of the 43 organizations to be interviewed by the committee itself. Two of the 15 declined; the committee then interviewed the remaining 13 firms.

In early 1970, the selection committee made a tentative choice and informed two organizations of their choice and of the probable percentage of The Common Fund portfolio that would be allocated to each. When the fund had obtained the necessary tax rulings from the Internal Revenue Service, in early 1971, the selection committee reviewed its tentative choice of managers, taking a look at the performance records of these two managers during 1970. The choice was allowed to stand, and when the fund began operations on July 1, 1971, its assets were divided approximately equally between the Capital Guardian Trust Company of Los Angeles and Massachusetts Financial Services of Boston. On February 1, 1972, The Common Fund hired two additional managers: Franklin Cole and Company and Mathers and Company. By this time, the fund had grown considerably, and the trustees had decided not to entrust more than about $50 million to any one manager, in order to achieve diversification of investment style. In July 1974, David L. Babson replaced Massachusetts Financial Services.

MULTIPLE MANAGERS

Particularly in the 1960s, pension funds, and to a lesser extent endowment funds, developed a tendency toward multiple management, using two, three, or sometimes as many as seven different managers. They had several reasons for believing that better investment results would follow from the use of more than one manager.

Perhaps the most common division of funds involves placing one manager in charge of fixed-income securities (primarily bonds) and another in charge of stocks, on the grounds that most managers specialize in one or the other, and few claim expertise in both. With this sort of rationale, a large fund might also use different managers for short-term and long-term portions of a fixed-income portfolio and for aggressive and defensive portions of a stock portfolio (or portions defined in other ways). In each case, the purpose is simply to make use of specialized skills.

A second reason for multiple managers is simply to achieve diversification. This rationale is a little harder to justify. One theory is that managers, especially "high-performance" managers, have good periods and bad periods. So by dividing its assets among several managers the fund reduces the risk that all the assets will be in the hands of a manager during one of his bad periods. Of course, it also reduces the chance of benefiting from good periods. Diversification as a safeguard against bad periods seems most appropriate when a fund has adopted a very aggressive policy involving a high degree of risk and has turned to very aggressive management. But having chosen high-risk and aggressive management, why should the fund then seek safety through multiple managers? It is not at all clear that several aggressive managers achieve better performance than one less aggressive manager, one less subject to good and bad periods. A more plausible approach to diversification involves the employment of managers taking different approaches to the selection of securities in order to produce a more fully diversified portfolio with some likelihood of above-average selection. But if substantial diversification of securities within the portfolio is an investment objective, then a single manager might accomplish all that a number of managers can.

Finally, some funds have turned to multiple management in the hope that competition among the managers, fostered partly by the promise that the best performer will be given a larger share of the funds to manage, will lead to better overall performance. There seems to be little evidence one way or the other as to the effectiveness of this approach.[27]

One result of a competitive arrangement is that one of the managers must report the lowest rate of return for each period, and the pressure to catch up, especially for a manager who had been last for several periods (not an unlikely position when results are published quarterly and a rise or decline in the market can persist for several quarters) can lead to irrational behavior and excessive risk taking. Some professionals predict this sort of behavior even before one manager has fallen behind, just as a result of the competitive environment. An investment committee might do well to think carefully about the behavior it would expect from each manager under conditions of competitive pressure.

Whether an institution employs one or several managers, switching managers is expensive. The new manager rarely wants to keep any of the old manager's securities. A 100 percent turnover in securities may cost from 2 to 10 percent in transaction costs, depending on whether the purchases and sales have an effect on prices. The breaking-in period is costly too, in terms of lost performance as the new manager settles in and begins to work with the committee.

TWO SPECIAL CASES: YALE AND HARVARD

Several universities with large endowments (including California, Chicago, Columbia, Rochester, and Texas) maintain their own investment staffs, but Yale and Harvard have come up with variations on this approach, which are worth special mention. Each university has established its own portfolio management company. In Yale's case, Endowment Management and Research Corporation (EM & R) is less than half-owned by Yale; it manages a mutual fund and has a number of clients apart from Yale. At Harvard, the Harvard Management Company, Inc., is a wholly owned subsidiary of the university and is concerned solely with the management of Harvard funds.

Until 1967, Yale's investments were handled by a three-man finance committee selected from the members of the Yale Corporation, assisted by a staff of university employees within the treasurer's office. In that year, the university organized EM & R, with 50 percent of its stock held by Yale and 50 percent by employees of the firm, and transferred to the firm the management of most of the Yale endowment fund. The reasoning behind the shift was described in the Treasurer's Annual Report for 1966–67.[28] Briefly, it was felt that the finance committee and the Yale treasurer's office could no longer carry the burden of actively managing a $500 million fund. And at the same time, the finance committee had determined on a significant change in investment style.

For a time previous, the finance committee considered the possibility of maintaining an investment staff at New Haven while turning over portions of the endowment portfolio to outside investment counsel. By early 1967, however, the committee had decided not to split the funds but to relocate the management outside New Haven, probably in New York City. At the same time, the committee concluded that it wanted a Yale organization to manage the endowment and anticipated establishing a staff of Yale employees in New York. The committee chose not to turn the endowment over to an independent organization, in part to avoid a conflict between the substantial Yale endowment and other funds the organization might be managing. They also wished to maintain for Yale some measure of control over the management organization and especially some familiarity with what was going on within that organization.

During the first quarter of 1967, Yale's new treasurer interviewed 40 or 50 individuals involved in many different kinds of investment management, soliciting opinions on the best form of investment organization for Yale. Then the committee began to narrow down the selection of those who would be asked to manage the endowment. Ultimately, the committee chose three men and decided that appropriate, tangible motivation called for a separate organization owned by the managers as well as by Yale. The result was EM & R, with its offices in Boston.

EM & R serves 32 corporate and endowment clients, besides Yale, and manages the Omega Fund, but the Yale endowment fund is the largest single fund under its management. Over the years, the Yale ownership in the firm has been reduced to about 40 percent, as employees of EM & R have purchased more stock.

In 1972, $75 million of the Yale endowment fund was transferred from EM & R to the management of T. Rowe Price and Associates, Inc., and a year later a second $75 million was placed under the management of the U.S. Trust Company of New York. The shifts were made on the recommendation of EM & R, so that Yale could benefit from diversification in investment styles.

At Harvard, the management of the endowment fund had for many years been quite unique. The Harvard treasurer had virtually complete control over investment management. Paul C. Cabot, treasurer from 1948 to 1965, and George F. Bennett, treasurer from 1965 to 1973, held simultaneously the offices of Harvard treasurer and chief executive officer of State Street Research and Management Co., and had the support of that institution's staff. In 1973, Harvard conducted much the same sort of analysis that Yale had some years earlier. Harvard considered the possibilities of creating an independent management company, building a management staff within the treasurer's office, and turning the portfolio over to one or several outside investment organizations. The result was the establishment of the Harvard Management Company, Inc. (HMC), as a wholly owned subsidiary of the university to deal exclusively with Harvard investments not in the hands of outside money managers. The Harvard financial report for 1973–74 described HMC as offering "the advantages of greater control and flexibility, a better understanding of the University's financial needs, freedom from the pressures of a profit-seeking organization, and finally, a method of management that is significantly less expensive than normal commercial fees."

THE COMMON FUND

The Common Fund is an endowment pool available only to educational institutions. Its original sponsors intended it as a solution to the problems of the institution with a small endowment fund in need of good management yet poorly equipped either to manage the fund internally or to find external management appropriate to its needs. They also hoped that The Common Fund might serve as an example to all educational institutions of how endowment funds should be managed.

The Common Fund is a nonprofit corporation, chartered by the New York State Legislature. During its early years, Teachers Insurance and Annuity Association assisted in the organization of its board of trustees, and it was financed by the Ford Foundation. The fund began its operations on July 1, 1971.

A member institution may join The Common Fund with an initial investment of $100,000 to $10 million as of any monthly entry date. The member institution purchases units in the pooled portfolio of The Common Fund, and the number of units purchased is simply the number of dollars invested divided by the unit value as of that date. (Appreciation or depreciation in the value of the portfolio is reflected by increases and decreases in the unit value.) Income is apportioned monthly on a unit basis and distributed quarterly, and an institution may withdraw funds with notice at the end of any month by cashing in its units at their month-end value. Except for the fact that investments and withdrawals must take place at month end, these procedures are similar to those followed by any mutual fund or educational endowment pool that uses the unit method of accounting. But The Common Fund does have some unique features.

First, it is itself tax-exempt. (Some uncertainties about its tax-exempt status were permanently removed by an amendment to the Internal Revenue Code in the summer of 1974.[29]) Second, the Fund does not have its own portfolio management organization; the trustees of The Common Fund are free to select the managers they think most appropriate. The managers are given full discretion over the funds committed to their care, subject to the investment objectives and policies established by the trustees of the fund. The investment objective is "the attainment of superior long-term total return, taking into account both appreciation and income, at an acceptable level of risk." The managers are expected to invest primarily in equities, but they are free to move to bonds or to cash equivalents when they feel that equities are overvalued.

The Common Fund offers a unique set of options to its members for the withdrawal of revenue for spending. For example, recognizing the preference of some institutions for spending only the dividend and interest income of an endowment fund. The Common Fund offers member institutions the option of withdrawing this income yield each quarter. A more popular option is quarterly withdrawal of a specific percentage of a 36-month moving average of the unit value. Under this option, the institution may withdraw and spend what it considers a prudent percentage of the market value of its endowment, an amount that may represent income yield solely or may include some appreciation and perhaps even some principal. The Common Fund suggests a quarterly withdrawal of 1.25 percent (a 5 percent annual rate) of the average value of a unit.

The fact that all the participants in The Common Fund are educational institutions may suggest a community of purpose that will keep the fund's objectives generally suitable for a college or university endowment fund. But clearly no single set of investment objectives will take care of the variety of needs of all colleges and universities. The Common Fund is one of a number of investment vehicles available to an institution. An investment committee will have to establish its own policy with respect to its total endowment and then decide how much, if any, of the funds to commit to The Common Fund. The Common Fund is essentially an equity vehicle, and most investment committees will find it appropriate to balance an investment in The Common Fund with an investment in fixed-income securities. There is no fixed-income pooled fund analogous to The Common Fund, although one is under consideration, but The Common Fund does have a separate fund for short-term investments.

As of June 1975, the total assets of The Common Fund pooled portfolio were about $119 million, and the membership consisted of 247 institutions.

COST OF INVESTING

Institutions that manage their endowment funds internally generally seem to feel that their management costs are lower than those institutions with external management. In some cases, they may be right, but it often appears that an institution does not really know what the costs of internal management are.

As institutions began to delegate the portfolio management function to outside professionals, they tended first to go to bank trust departments, which, by and large, charged quite modest fees. Fees under 0.25 percent per year of the value of assets managed are still not uncommon. Those institutions that became dissatisfied with banks as portfolio managers and turned to investment counseling firms, as many did in the late 1960s, found that these firms charged considerably more. Fees ranging from 0.15 percent per year to 1 percent per year are fairly common. The statistics collected by the Harris Survey in 1971 show that for the reported colleges and universities that made use of outside management, the managers' fees ranged from 0.1 percent of assets managed to 0.75 percent per year.[30] For 22 institutions visited by the author in 1968, fees ranged from 0.01 percent to 0.75 percent. Some recent data on fund management costs (not necessarily for endowment funds) suggest average fees for $10 million accounts of 0.52 percent for investment counselors managing small accounts, 0.44 percent for counselors managing larger accounts, 0.36 percent for brokerage firms and investment subsidiaries of banks, and 0.22 percent for bank trust departments. To some extent, the differences in fees represent differences in the number of accounts handled by each individual portfolio officer in the management organization. Investment counseling firms favor few clients per manager and, for this reason, will not accept small accounts. A minimum-sized account from $5 million to $25 million is common. Bank trust officers generally carry the heaviest loads. Some banks may charge low fees in the hope of being made custodian for a fund and earning further fees for this service.

In addition to management fees, the costs associated with an

endowment fund include: custodianship fees (for safekeeping of securities), professional fees (legal and accounting), administrative costs,
and transactions costs (brokerage fees). The experience of The
Common Fund may serve as a guide to the share of total assets that
these costs may represent. Table 2-1 shows these figures for the year
ending June 30, 1974. The fund regards total annual expenses of
0.48 percent of average assets as normal and assesses participants at
this rate.[31]

Transactions costs have long been ignored or at least paid scant
attention to in establishing an investment policy and measuring performance. But if the cost of a "round trip" (purchase and sale) is
estimated at between 2 percent and 10 percent of the value of the
securities bought and sold (the cost will depend to some extent on the
impact of the transactions on prices), then portfolio turnover of only
10 percent will lead to transactions costs between 0.2 percent and 1
percent of the total portfolio. Measured against the 0.48 percent that
is expected to cover *all* of The Common Fund's other expenses, turnover and transactions costs begin to emerge as important considerations in investment policy.

Before May 1, 1975, commission rates on transactions under
$300,000 were fixed, and institutions could not shop around, at least
within the stock exchange membership, for reduced costs. Brokers
competed by offering a variety of services, including performance
measurements, in exchange for commission business at the fixed
rates. Roughly one-third of the commission was regarded as available
to purchase these services. Colleges and universities displayed widely
varying degrees of effectiveness in making use of this competition.
Some obtained valuable service; some allowed their managers to have
the benefits of the commission buying power. (Of the $685,000 in

**Table 2-1   Expenses of The Common Fund, Year Ending
June 30, 1974**

	EXPENSE ($)	AVERAGE ASSETS (%)
Investment managers' fees	528,066	0.32
Custodian & record keeping	130,101	0.08
Legal, accounting, auditing, and other consulting services	174,793*	0.11
Administration	149,288	0.09
Trustee fees & expenses	37,759	0.02
Total	1,020,007*	0.61

*$125,093 for legal services, representing 0.08 percent of average assets, was largely committed to
the one-time establishment of the fund's tax-exempt status.

brokerage commissions it paid in the year ending June 30, 1974, The Common Fund used $200,000 to purchase services beyond the purchase and sale transactions.)

Now that commission rates are negotiable, institutions may choose between continuing to use commissions to purchase services other than securities transactions and purchasing these services separately. Investment committees and managers also must balance price and quality of service to determine where transactions will be handled. Brokers, faced for the first time with genuine price competition, have had great difficulty in establishing rates, and institutions, as of mid-1975, have faced further difficulty in determining what are reasonable rates. Clearly, rates for institutions have fallen well below the old fixed rates—at least 25 percent and perhaps as much as 40 percent below.

During the 1960s, a number of colleges and universities experienced difficulties in allocating brokerage transactions. The high fixed rates made all brokerage profitable, and many alumni suggested that their continued support entitled them to a share of their institution's business. The problem seems to have become less serious, perhaps because institutions have learned to deal with it. The most satisfactory solution seems to be to direct all applicants to the portfolio manager, who is expected to allocate brokerage entirely on the basis of the value of services rendered and the commissions paid. Public relations concerns may call for some exceptions to this rule, but the exceptions generally create further problems.

DOES THE FORM OF MANAGEMENT MATTER?

The move to external portfolio measurement and the preference for investment counseling firms, despite their generally higher fees, imply some hope for improved investment performance. And two studies have concluded that external management of endowment funds does achieve superior results. One of these studies, by Harold A. Davidson, was reported in *The Financial Analysts Journal* in early 1971.[32]

Professor Davidson based his conclusions on a questionnaire survey and reported that for 116 institutions, for the 10-year period from 1957–67, the average annual rate of capital appreciation was 4.88 percent on externally managed funds and 3.51 percent on internally managed funds and the average annual income yield was 4.82 percent and 4.51 percent, respectively. These statistics are somewhat suspect; my own experience indicates that in 1967 very few educational institutions were in a position to calculate the investment performance of their endowment funds accurately for that year, let alone the preceding nine years.[33] At that time, most institutions were relying on book values rather than market values for all of their measurements, and a number of them were unable to distinguish growth due to contributions from growth due to investment performance.

The Harris Associates Survey, covering 10 years (presumably ending in 1970), reported an average annual rate of return of 5.6 percent for the funds using outside managers and 4.7 percent for the internally managed funds.[34] This "average rate of return" was apparently a rate of appreciation, because the report goes on to say that the yield on internally managed funds was 7.8 percent. Now, if these are average yields over a 10-year period, then they were almost certainly based upon book values and not on market values. It would have taken extraordinary efforts at maximizing current income to produce an average yield of 8.1 percent based on market values over the decade. Even if the reported yield applied only to the end of the 10-year period, it seems very unlikely that the yield figures are computed on market value. These inconsistencies cast doubt on whether the 5.6 and 4.7 percent figures are correct measures of investment performance.

I have found almost no correlation from one time period to another in rankings of funds by investment performance. In other words, while one can easily rank a number of funds or a number of managers on the basis of performances achieved over one time period (which might be 5 or 10 years), this ranking would provide no guidance whatever to the probable ranking in any future period.[35] This conclusion is not inconsistent with the proposition that a few managers have superior ability, perhaps not very much better than the abilities of other managers but at least somewhat better, and that all other managers are pretty much the same. I reported evidence that some mutual funds are consistently in the top 40 percent of their industry in performance, but it has not proved possible to identify any truly outstanding managers.

III / Investment Performance: Evaluating Results and Forecasting the Future

There are four principal reasons for evaluating the investment performance of an endowment fund:

First, the investment committee, and ultimately the board of trustees, bears the responsibility of seeing to it that the fund is managed according to agreed-on investment objectives.

Second, comparisons of the performance of the endowment fund with the performances of other endowment funds—or other professionally managed capital—may help to determine whether the abilities of managers differ significantly. If they do, then the investment committee can be sensitive to the possible need and opportunity for a change in management.

Third, by searching for relationships between good or bad performance and other characteristics of a fund or its management, the investment committee may find ways to improve performance.

Finally, a review of the performance of an endowment over a significant period of time, and of the performances of endowments generally, can provide some insights into probable long-run performance which have important implications for investment policy and spending policy.

MEASUREMENT OF PERFORMANCE

Colleges and universities have been notorious for investing very large sums of money and producing only very crude measures, if any, of what happened to these sums. They have been among the last of the institutional investors to establish systematic and reasonably scientific measures of investment performance.[1]

The most obvious aspect of investment performance is the rate of profit or return. The "total return" is the sum of the appreciation in value—or growth—in the endowment, and its income yield (dividends, interest, and the like). Growth, yield, and total return are usually expressed in percentage terms, so that if a fund has appreciated in value from $1,000,000 to $1,045,000 and has produced $55,000 in dividends and interest income, it has shown growth of 4.5 percent, yield of 5.5 percent, and total return of 10.0 percent.

The values from which a growth rate is deduced are market values—the values at which the portfolio securities are currently quoted or at which they could be sold. The term "book value," often used in discussions of endowment, simply records the prices of all the securities in a portfolio as of the time when they were added, plus realized gains and losses. Although book value is the conventional figure used for describing an endowment fund on an institution's balance sheet, it is of no use in calculating investment performance.

The increase in market value of an endowment fund represents investment growth only if there have been no additions to or withdrawals from the endowment during the period being measured. This is often the case for separately invested funds, but not for pooled funds. Most endowments consist of pooled funds with occasional additions and withdrawals, and the usual method of identifying growth due solely to investment performance is to place the endowment on a unit basis, like a mutual fund.[2] Thus, the value of a unit records the investment performance, while the number of units varies with the addition or withdrawal of capital.

The use of units valued at market, both for performance measurement and for income allocation, is essential for adequate supervision of a pooled endowment.[3] Briefly, the procedure for unitizing a pooled fund is to select a convenient unit value—$10 or $100 perhaps—and to divide the market value of the pool by this value to obtain the total number of units. If, for example, the unit value is set at $10 and the market value of the endowment is $1,000,000, then the number of units is 100,000. When a gift is added to the pooled fund, the number of new units is simply the value of the gift divided by the unit value on the date it enters the pool. At a $10 unit value, a gift of $25,000 is credited with 2,500 units, and the total number of units in the pool becomes 102,500. Because under this system, the unit value is affected only by investment performance, it can serve as an accurate measure of growth. And the value of a particular gift can be determined by multiplying the current unit value by the number of units attributable to the gift. The unit system also makes it easy to determine what share of total pool income belongs to the gift fund.

Unit values and unit income figures make possible the calculation of the growth, yield, and total return of a fund, but a few problems remain. One concerns the time at which income was received. Consider two funds each of which has a unit value of $10 at the beginning of a year and $10.40 at the end of the year and an income per unit of $0.50. For each, the growth is 4 percent and the income yield 5 percent, for a total return of 9 percent based on the original $10 value. But this calculation assumes that the income was received at the end of the year. If one fund got its income at year end and the other received it during the year, the latter performed better than the former, either making income available for reinvestment or eliminating the need to borrow funds for operations during the rest of the year. Some techniques permit exact calculations without assumptions as to the time of receipt of income.[4] But if the calculation covers a period no longer than a month, these refinements are probably not necessary.

Rates of return may also be calculated on a "time-weighted" or a "dollar-weighted" basis. The dollar-weighted rate, known as the "internal rate of return" to those who analyze capital investment decisions, is a good measure of the experience of the institution with its endowment but is not as good a measure of the manager's achievement as is the time-weighted total return rate. Again, if the basic time period is no longer than a month, these refinements are probably not necessary and the difference between time-weighted and dollar-weighted rates of return is inconsequential.[5]

A final problem arises when the rates of return for a number of months are combined into an average rate for a longer period—a quarter or a year or several years. Consider two months, for which the total return rates on a fund are +12 and −8 percent. The arithmetic average of the two rates, which is 2 percent per month, does not accurately reflect what has happened to this fund. Its history, assuming it began with a value of $100, consists of a rise to $112 and then a decline to $103. A sum of $100 that grows to $103 at the end of two months is growing at a compound average rate of 1.5 percent per month, which is the geometric or compound average of the +12 and −8 percent rates.[6] It can be calculated for any number of months, and from it can be deduced quarterly, semiannual, and annual rates of return. The compound average growth rate or total-return rate is the correct measure of growth or of the total-return experience of a fund over a series of time periods. (Simply averaging the yield rates for several periods does not provide any useful record of performance.)

The most useful rate-of-return figure in evaluating the overall investment performance of a fund and comparing it to that of other funds is almost certainly the total return or average total return over several periods. One must be sure that it is, in fact, total returns that are being compared. Most bond and stock indexes are price indexes, recording appreciation but not income yield. One must adjust for yield to arrive at a total-return figure.

MEASURES OF RISK

Rate of return, however well measured, is only one dimension of investment performance. A second is risk. In the hope of achieving profits or returns, investors take risks. In the hope of achieving extraordinary returns, they take extraordinary risks. When they are successful and their high returns are compared with the more modest results of a conservative investment strategy, it is appropriate to allow for this difference in risk taking and not to credit the superior rate of return entirely to superior judgment. But an acceptable quantitative measure of risk is difficult to establish.

Webster defines "risk" as "the possibility of loss." The greater the likelihood of loss and the greater the size of the possible loss, the greater the risk. It is difficult to put a number on this kind of risk, but it is necessary to do so if some judgment is to be made as to the appropriate risk level for an endowment portfolio or the permissible risk of individual securities in it.

The academic community has developed statistical measures for this purpose. These measures are far from perfect, but one need not accept all of the claims put forward for them in order to derive some benefit from them.[7]

Statistical measures of risk are generally based on the assumption that if all the *possible* results of an investment, from best to worst, are pictured as a range or distribution of outcomes, then the distribution contains a picture of the risk. If the investment is very safe—a savings account, for example—the outcome for the next quarter is pretty well known and the range or distribution of possible outcomes is very narrow. The best and worst possible outcomes will not be far apart. A highly speculative investment, on the other hand, offers a wide distribution of possible outcomes. The two situations are contrasted in Figure 3-1.

Despite the relationship between the likelihood and size of loss and the statistical risk measures, the validity of the measures is open to question. First, they usually are based on *past* outcomes and on the assumption that these past outcomes are a fair sample of the outcomes that could be expected in the future. But past outcomes—the annual

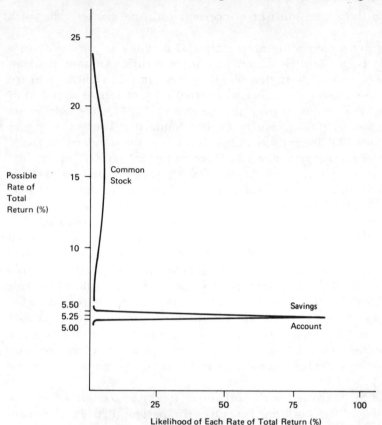

Figure 3-1. Investment Uncertainty

rates of return actually achieved on an investment over the past decade, for example—are *not* always indicative of what can be anticipated from this investment in the future. Second, the risk measures
do not necessarily reflect the real distribution of possible future outcomes. For example, risk measures generally assume a symmetrical
distribution, which implies that the likelihood of an outcome far *below*
the most probable outcome is about the same as that of an outcome
far *above* the most probable. Any other assumption leads to great
mathematical complexity.

    In fact, what are called "statistical measures of risk" are really
measures of variability in return. Although these measures do not
fully reflect what an investor's intuition may indicate is "risk," variability is an important component of risk, and the measures are especially

useful to those who must be concerned with the market value of a portfolio.

The most commonly used statistical measure of variability in a portfolio is standard deviation in rate of return. Another is mean absolute deviation.[8] Both describe the spread in a distribution and are usually computed from a series of actual rates of return achieved in the past. For example, over the 48 years 1926–73, the arithmetic average annual rate of return on the Standard & Poor's Composite Index (the "500" Index) was 11.6 percent, and the standard deviation of those 48 rates of return was 21.9 percent. If the rates of return over those years are a fair indication of the return on the Standard & Poor's 500 Index in any particular year, then the distribution of possible rates of return may be characterized by a mean or most likely return of 11.6 percent and a standard deviation, measuring the spread of the distribution, of 21.9 percent. In assuming a normal distribution, one anticipates that in only one year in six will the return be more than one standard deviation below the expected value, that is, below −10.3 percent, and in only one year in six will it be above 33.5 percent; in the other four years, one expects the return to fall somewhere between −10.3 and 33.5 percent. And in only 5 years out of 200 should the rate fall more than two standard deviations below the expected value, that is, to −32 percent or lower. (In fact, the Standard & Poor's 500 has lost more than 32 percent in 2 years out of the past 50.)

The Standard & Poor's 500 Index might be considered as representative of the stock market. Over the period 1926–73, the arithmetic average return on treasury bills was about 2.2 percent per year. Although the stock market was more profitable than were treasury bills, it also was more variable. Its average "excess return" over the treasury bill rate was 11.6 % − 2.2% = 9.4% a year, and it displayed a variability, measured by standard deviation, of 21.9 percent. Assuming treasury bills to be completely stable (with a standard deviation of 0 percent), we can deduce an excess return per unit of variability for the stock market as (11.6% − 2.2%)/21.9% = 0.43% . This formula measures the "efficiency" of the stock market as an investment vehicle over the period 1926–73. It offered 0.43 percent a year in total return over the rate available on a quite stable or risk-free investment, per percentage point of variability. This standard can be used to judge actual portfolio performance.

If a particular portfolio achieved and average total return of 14 percent a year over the period 1926–73, with a standard deviation of 28 percent, its efficiency can be expressed as (14% − 2.2%)/28% = 0.42. The portfolio was slightly less efficient than the market;

although more profitable than the market as a whole, it involved a disproportionately higher variability. Consider two portfolios, one with a total return averaging 13 percent with a standard deviation of 21 percent and another averaging 9 percent with a standard deviation of 13.3 percent. Each has an efficiency measure of 0.51 and can be considered superior to the market (with an efficiency of 0.43) and to the first portfolio (with an efficiency of 0.42), in overall performance.

Figure 3-2 is a graph of the total return of The Common Fund over the first 48 months of its existence (July 1971–June 1975), plotted against the total return on the Standard & Poor's 500 Index. The graph shows that the fund followed the stock market index rather closely. The Common Fund's arithmetic average monthly rate of return over the period was 0.1 percent per month, and its efficiency was

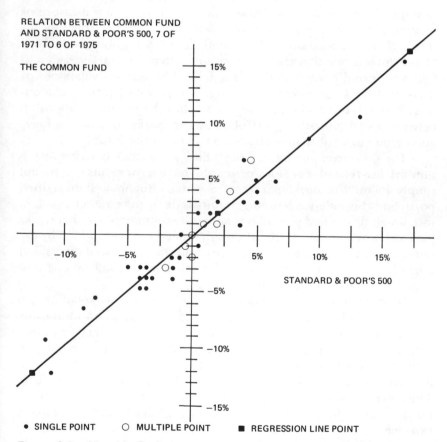

RELATION BETWEEN COMMON FUND
AND STANDARD & POOR'S 500, 7 OF
1971 TO 6 OF 1975

THE COMMON FUND

STANDARD & POOR'S 500

• SINGLE POINT   ○ MULTIPLE POINT   ■ REGRESSION LINE POINT

Figure 3-2. Monthly Performance of The Common Fund and the Standard & Poor's 500 Index, July 1971–June 1975

−0.075. For the Standard & Poor's 500 Index itself, the arithmetic average monthly rate of return was 0.3 percent a month, and its efficiency was −0.033. Hence the fund was a little less efficient than the market.

MARKET RISK AND INDEPENDENT VARIABILITY

The uncertainty surrounding the future performance of a common stock has two components. One is market-related uncertainty. Almost all common stocks rise when the stock market as a whole rises and fall when the market falls. Most common stock portfolios also rise and fall with the market. One can compare the performance of a stock or portfolio with that of the market as a whole (as represented, for example, by a broad stock market index) and deduce a measure of their relationship that is sometimes referred to as the "volatility" of the stock or portfolio or its "beta coefficient." A highly volatile stock or portfolio is one that rises very rapidly when the market rises and falls very rapidly when the market falls. The historic volatilities of individual stocks provide only a rough indication of future relationships between the stocks and the market, but the historic relationship between a well-diversified portfolio and the market is usually a fairly good guide to what that relationship will be in the future.

The other component of uncertainty as to stock performance is non-market-related. For stock prices also have movements that do not simply follow the stock market as a whole. But in well-diversified portfolios, this independent uncertainty is likely to be rather small; in fact, a well-diversified portfolio is almost by definition one that tracks the stock market very closely, although it need not rise and fall by the same amount that the market rises and falls. (A well-diversified portfolio with a volatility of 1.5 will both rise and fall by one and one-half times as much as the market.)

If an endowment portfolio is well diversified, its volatility can serve as an indication of how the portfolio will perform under any market conditions. History may provide a guide to the likely extremes of behavior in the stock market as a whole, and these figures, combined with the portfolio's volatility, provide the basis for a deduction as to the likely extremes of performance of the endowment portfolio. These extremes may be compared with the tolerance of the institution for declines in the value of a portfolio which will probably accompany extreme declines in the market. Volatility thus helps to describe the tolerable risk level in the endowment portfolio.

Figure 3-3 shows the total rate of return on the University of

Rochester endowment fund and the return on the Standard & Poor's 500 Index plotted for the 10 years 1965–74. A line of best fit through the 10 points shows the approximate relationship between the 10 annual performances of the endowment fund and those of the market. The slope of the line (the volatility or beta), corresponding to the market risk, is 1.01, which means that the fund return rises and falls a little more than the market itself.

The points plotted in Figure 3-3 are clustered approximately around the line, but they are somewhat dispersed. The fund tracks

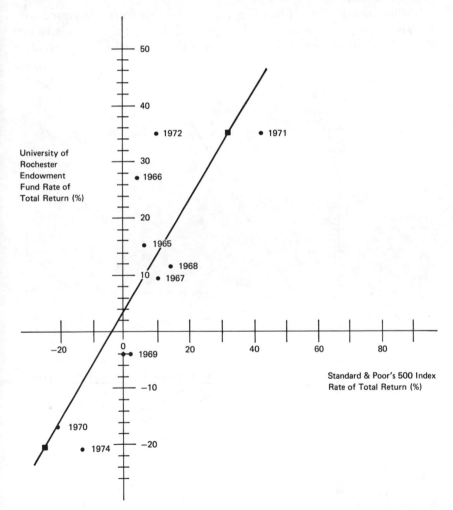

Figure 3-3. Endowment Fund Performance, University of Rochester, 1965-74

the market only fairly closely. This dispersion reflects the aspects of the fund's performance record that cannot then be explained by the movement of the market, as represented by the Standard & Poor's 500 Index. This additional uncertainty is the portfolio's unique or independent variability.

Figure 3-4 shows a similar graph for another endowment fund, Fund E11. In this case, the slope of the line of best fit is only 0.97 and the points lie very close to the line. This fund seems to track the Standard & Poor's 500 Index very faithfully and shows little independent variability.

The volatility of a fund is a more attractive variability measure than is an overall measure like the standard deviation, in part because it can be derived and illustrated in graph form, which has greater

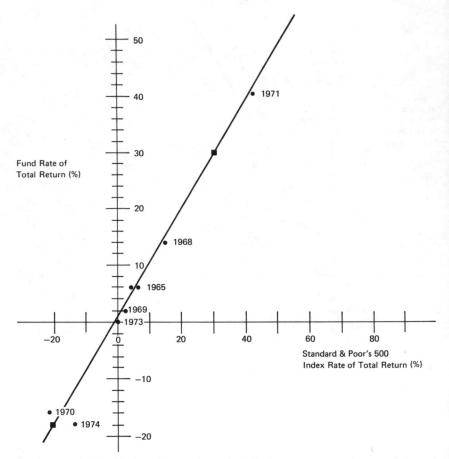

Figure 3-4. Endowment Fund Performance Fund E11, 1965–74

intuitive appeal than does a pure statistic computed by a formula from a series of rates of return. But perhaps even more important is the fact that, however skeptical one may be about statistical measures of risk, volatility and graphs depicting it may still prove useful in predicting the performance of a fund under any particular market conditions. Figure 3-4 is more useful than Figure 3-3 for this purpose: Fund E11, whose performance it illustrates, is more diversified than the University of Rochester endowment and has less independent variability (independent variability also is referred to as "diversifiable variability"), and its volatility is a more complete statistical description of its risk. Like standard deviation, volatility can be used in combination with the rate of return to derive an overall performance-quality measure.[9]

Generally speaking, a fund must be pretty well diversified for volatility to serve as a useful risk measure and for the graph to be a good predictor of performance under different market conditions. This is the case for a great many pooled funds.[10]

These two kinds of variability measure—overall measures, such as standard deviation, and measures of market risk, such as volatility—have become widely accepted among academic writers and businessmen. But they are still criticized by some commentators who do not perceive them as an accurate reflection of what their intuition tells them is the risk in a portfolio. In particular, the critics correctly point out that these measures depend largely on historical relationships that will not necessarily persist. But the measures are more useful than anything else presently available to trustees for measuring both risk and return together to arrive at an overall *quality* evaluation rather than a simple, one-dimensional growth figure. And volatility, which is the more widely used and accepted measure, has the further virtue of helping forecast performance, whether or not it truly measures risk.

EVALUATION OF PARTICULAR FUNDS' PERFORMANCE

In setting objectives for an endowment fund, trustees should specify the level of risk—preferably in terms of a target range of volatility. Once an acceptable range has been determined, trustees should monitor the actual volatility and, when encountering deviations, call for an explanation from the investment manager. Trustees can also go on to use one of the efficiency measures discussed above to evaluate overall performance, comparing that of the fund with that of an index—with the index representing an average unmanaged portfolio involving no skill or judgment—or with that of other funds. As a practical matter, although checking volatilities against a target volatility level is a fairly common practice, the use of measures of efficiency is still largely restricted to academic analysts. The risk measures that underly the efficiency measures have not yet inspired enough confidence for many professional investors to accept the efficiency measures as valid performance criteria.[11]

Statistical measures can be used also to evaluate two specific aspects of a manager's performance: selection and timing. Skill in timing enables a manager to enter the stock market when prices are low and to retreat to cash when prices are high. It may also extend to moving among different classes of stocks and different classes of bonds, buying the classes that are low and selling those that are high. If a manager is left free or is even encouraged to follow his judgment in making moves of this sort, then his success or failure at it is a matter of concern. Techniques for measuring success and failure in timing in essence compare the manager's results to the results that a policy of unchanging distribution of holdings between cash and stocks or among different classes of stocks and bonds would have achieved.

Skill in selection involves purchase of the best stocks when stocks are bought at all or of the best stocks of a class when that class is bought. Virtually every manager is expected to make use of this skill, but if he is to exercise other skills, such as timing, at the same time, special measurements may be necessary for identification of success or failure at selection. These measurements generally consist of comparisons between the manager's performance and what would have been accomplished by following the same timing the manager actually used but purchasing an average or random set of securities in the class he purchased (for example, growth stocks, long-term bonds) rather than the particular securities he chose.[12]

Managers or performance-measurement services (or the financial officers of a college or university, using the institution's own facilities) can make all of these measurements. But most investment committees still rely on simple rate-of-return comparisons between their funds and others with similar characteristics. In principle, there is nothing wrong with these comparisons except that the set of truly comparable funds may turn out to be so small that comparisons become useless. As a practical matter, it is difficult to tell whether all of the funds in a set presented for comparison really are comparable. Trustees who make rate-of-return comparisons and who let their managers know they are doing so, without very careful control over true comparability, may be encouraging the managers to strive for higher returns by taking higher risks than the trustees really want.

Performance data for pension funds, mutual funds, bank and

insurance company funds, and other endowment funds are available for comparison purposes. A number of services, to be purchased for cash or brokerage commissions,[13] provide sets of purportedly comparable data and carry out the comparisons.

The trouble with comparisons to pension fund performances is that the particular pension funds are never identified and their risk levels and investment objectives are generally not disclosed. The validity of the comparison generally rests on an assurance that the pension funds being compared are all of about the same size as the endowment fund in question. But size does not appear to be as closely related to investment performance as are risk and investment objectives.[14]

Mutual funds, however, can be identified, their investment objectives learned, and their risk evaluated. The trouble with using mutual funds for the purpose of comparison is that relatively few mutual funds appear to be truly comparable with a particular endowment fund. Mutual funds are generally operated for the benefit of taxpaying investors rather than tax-exempt institutions; they are therefore not quite as free as are tax-exempt funds to take advantage of investment opportunities. So a tax-exempt fund, such as an endowment fund, should do a little better than a mutual fund. The Common Fund is, in effect, a pooled fund for colleges and universities, and its performance may be comparable to that of an endowment fund.[15]

Comparisons to other endowment funds may seem the most appropriate, but even they present difficulties. Colleges and universities are still shy about disclosing their endowment fund performances data; and the most complete set of endowment fund performance data, collected by the investment committee of the National Association of College and University Business Officers (NACUBO), which prepares comparative performance analyses and supplies them to participating institutions,[16] is recorded under code names. This practice makes an appraisal of comparability impossible. But the funds are classified by size (for what it is worth) and by percent invested in equities (which gives some insight into investment objectives). Some of the comparative analyses include volatilities, giving a further indication of objectives and risk level. It may be particularly important to know the investment objectives of endowment funds that are being compared, since some are run as pension funds, without any preference for either growth or income, while others are heavily influenced by a preference for current income.

Performance records for endowment funds generally are derived from figures calculated within the accounting departments of colleges and universities and are not subject to independent audit. Some of the data submitted in the NACUBO annual survey are clearly erroneous and can be excluded from comparative statistics. But other errors may easily slip by. Most of the performance-measurement services, which provide pension fund statistics for the most part, also are capable of error. But endowment fund comparisons are particularly vulnerable to inaccuracies.

DIFFERENCES IN PERFORMANCE AMONG FUNDS

The assumptions that justify comparisons of investment performance among funds or managers are that performance quality differs from fund to fund and that the measures of performance are valid reflections of these differences. Unfortunately, the two assumptions cannot be tested independently, but evidence as to their joint validity can be found in some tests run on endowment funds and on mutual funds over the 10-year period ending June 30, 1974.

The tests were first run on 158 mutual funds (most of them included in the set for which *Barron's* publishes quarterly performance data and in the performance comparisons sent to institutions participating in the NACUBO performance studies). The funds were ranked from 1 to 158 on the basis of efficiency of performance over the five years ending June 30, 1969, and again over the succeeding five years ended June 30, 1974. Efficiency in this case was calculated as excess return over risk-free rate divided by total variability as measured by standard deviation. A comparison of the rankings for the two periods showed no significant correlation.[17] Another efficiency ranking, based on rate of return and volatility, yielded the same results.[18] In short, the efficiency measures based on the first five years were useless in predicting efficiency in the second five years.

These findings suggest either that the efficiency measures were not valid or that the funds did not differ in efficiency from one another. The findings were not inconsistent with the proposition that although *most* mutual funds are about equal in quality, there are a few superior ones and perhaps a few inferior ones. But this proposition would be very difficult to test.

Although the tests above did not reveal a consistent ranking in quality among mutual funds, a similar test using total variability, represented by standard deviation in rate of return, as the criterion of ranking showed a fairly high correlation between the two five-year periods.[19] That is, on the basis of variability in performance, the ranking of the funds over the first five years provided a good guide to their ranking over the second five years, even though rankings by *efficiency* had no predictive value.

These tests were applied also to 67 endowment funds (all the funds for which 10 years of data were available). On the basis of efficiency measured as excess return over a risk-free rate per unit of standard deviation, the correlation was low but positive.[20] On the basis of efficiency measured as rate of return combined with volatility, the correlation was still modest but a little higher.[21] These findings suggest that the quality of endowment fund management varies more than does that of mutual fund management—a plausible conclusion given the variety of ways in which endowment funds are managed.

The state of the art is not yet such as to permit confident identification of superior management. It seems particularly difficult, if not impossible, to rate the performance of the professionals who manage mutual funds. It seems somewhat less difficult to rate the performance of endowment funds. In light of these findings, the trustees or investment committee of an institution may find it useful to compare the performance of their endowment with that of other endowments (and other funds generally), but it seems unlikely that they will succeed in identifying the best-performing professional manager. It seems more important to establish appropriate objectives and to find a manager who will achieve them than to search for a high-performance manager.

PERFORMANCE-RELATED CHARACTERISTICS

Table 3-1 shows a number of characteristics of endowment funds for the 10 years ending June 30, 1974 (a "poor" period for the stock market) and for the 10 ending June 30, 1972 (a "good" period). Fund size and rate of return showed some correlation. For the decade ending in 1972, the larger funds outperformed the smaller funds with one exception: the $50 million to $100 million class outperformed the over $100 million class. As one might expect over this time period, a high rate of return generally went with high volatility. The exception is the $10 million to $25 million class, with relatively high volatility and a modest return. The average percent invested in equities did not seem to correlate with either volatility or rate of return. But this average is as of June 30, 1974, and may have little to do with performance through 1972.

For the decade ending in 1974, size seems to have had less to do with performance than it had for the decade ending in 1972, but the $50 million to $100 million funds still made up the highest rate-of-return class and high returns tended to be associated with large size. One might expect for this period of poor stock market performance that high volatility would have been associated with low rates of re-

Table 3-1   Performance Characteristics of Endowment Funds

10 Years to June 30, 1974

NUMBER OF FUNDS	SIZE CLASS*	AVERAGE TOTAL RETURN (%)	AVERAGE PERCENT IN EQUITIES*	AVERAGE VOLATILITY
14	Over $100 million	3.03	60	0.67
10	$50–$100 million	3.28	70	0.78
11	$25–$50 million	3.23	63	0.58
17	$10–$25 million	2.04	63	0.79
27	Under $10 million	2.99	62	0.60
79	Standard & Poor's 500 Index	3.85		1.00

10 Years to June 30, 1972

14	Over $100 million	8.17	63	0.63
10	$50–$100 million	8.55	72	0.66
12	$25–$50 million	7.40	62	0.55
17	$10–$25 million	7.03	63	0.71
22	Under $10 million	6.85	61	0.55
75	Standard & Poor's 500 Index	10.49		1.00

*Size used for each fund, for both decades, is as of June 30, 1974. Percent invested in equities is also as of June 30, 1974.
Source: National Association of College and University Business Officers (NACUBO) data.

turn. But both the highest and lowest rate-of-return classes had about the same volatility. And the other three classes showed no consistent pattern. The volatility of funds over the decade did show some correlation with percent invested in equities as of June 30, 1974, except for funds of the $10 to $25 million class.

In general, no strong relationships are evident, but one might conclude that large endowment funds tend to be more profitable than small ones, that volatility is associated with percent invested in equities, and that high volatility has accompanied high rates of return in good markets and is not clearly associated with low rates of return in poor markets.

LONG-RUN PERFORMANCE EXPECTATIONS

The numerous studies of the long-run performance record of the bond and stock markets can serve as a guide to rates of return that can be obtained by simply "buying the market." As a practical matter, few individuals have enough money to buy a cross section of the stock or bond market, but a substantial endowment fund can do so. The Index Fund of America, a mutual fund for tax-exempt institutions, located in San Francisco, estimates that a $70 million fund can economically hold the 500 stocks in the Standard & Poor's Index, in proportions corresponding to the index. And a much smaller fund can approximate the index. Of course, buying a cross section of the market involves transaction costs that would bring the rate of return on a portfolio below the rate calculated on a market index. But the index is "unmanaged," and one might hope that a skillful manager who did not simply buy the market would achieve a performance good enough to at least offset transaction costs (and cover management fees), so that the fund would do as well as the market as a whole.

Probably the best-known study of the performance of the stock market is the one by Lawrence Fisher and James H. Lorie, who computed the month-by-month rate of return, from 1926 through 1965, that would have been achieved by an investor who had held every stock on the New York Stock Exchange over that period.[22] And the best-known figure relating to the same subject is the compound or geometric average rate of total return (appreciation plus dividends) over that entire period: 9.3 percent per year. This number has been taken by many investors as a guide to long-run rates of return on common stocks.

During the 1926–65 period, the average annual rate of inflation as represented by the Consumer Price Index of the Bureau of Labor Statistics was about 1.5 percent per year. So Fisher and Lorie's compound-rate-of-return figure, corrected for inflation, becomes about 7.8 percent per year (9.3 percent − 1.5 percent).

In 1974, an analysis of rates of return on common stocks, long-term high-grade bonds, and treasury bills, for the period 1926–73, was reported by Roger G. Ibbotson and Rex A. Sinquefield.[23] This analysis was based upon published and computed indexes rather than upon the performances of individual stocks, and it was not nearly as exhaustive as the Fisher and Lorie study. But for purposes of practical forecasting, it is probably more useful. Table 3-2 summarizes several of the conclusions of the study. The table shows, for three classes of investments, for the period 1926–73, the compound average return, the standard deviation (which is a measure of the year-to-year variability in the rate of return), and the compound average annual "real" return (which reflects the 2 percent per year average inflation over this period, as represented by the Consumer Price Index). All of the rates of return embrace both appreciation and dividends or interest. (The

Table 3-2   Rates of Return, 1926–73

	GEOMETRIC AVERAGE ANNUAL RATE OF RETURN (%)		STANDARD DEVIATION IN RATE OF RETURN (%)	GEOMETRIC AVERAGE REAL ANNUAL RATE OF RETURN (%)	
Standard & Poor's Composite (500) Common Stock Index	9.3	(8.4)*	21.9	7.3	(6.2)
Long-term high-grade bonds	3.6	(3.5)	5.0	1.6	(1.3)
Treasury bills	2.2	(2.3)	1.8	0.2	(0.1)
Rate of inflation	2.0	(2.2)			

*Figures in parentheses are updated to cover 1926–74.

Source: National Association of College and University Business Officers (NACUBO) data.

updated figures are the authors.) The compound average rate of return is a good measure of the profitability of an investment. But the compound average real rate of return is an even more useful figure.

The period 1926–65 includes enormous variety in economic conditions and stock market performance. Some experts maintain that the depression of the 1930s was a unique event, the experience of which should not be built into any long-run forecast. But others point out that the great bull market of the 1950s and early 1960s was equally remarkable. In the author's opinion, the full 1926–65 period studied by Fisher and Lorie is useful for prediction purposes. Ibbotson and Sinquefield, who extended the period of their study to 1973—a poor year for common stocks—ended up with an average real return over the full period (7.3 percent) which was not very different from the average real return found by Fisher and Lorie (7.8 percent). The 6.2 percent real return for 1926–74 is probably an extreme, out of the range of reasonable expectations. These findings suggest that a reasonable forecast for real returns in the long run on common stocks is around 7 to 8 percent a year.

The Ibbotson and Sinquefield work indicates a compound average real rate of return for long-term high-grade bonds of 1.6 percent a year. This and a number of other studies of long-term interest rates suggest a long-run geometric average real total return of 1 to 3 percent on long-term bonds. These historic data come, in part, from a period before the Treasury–Federal Reserve "accord" of 1951, by which yields on United States government bonds were "pegged" by the Federal Reserve. Some experts would argue that the data from this period are misleading, suggesting returns on bonds that are lower, relative to stock returns, than can be expected for the future. There is indeed evidence of a real average yield on high-grade corporate bonds of 3 to 3.5 percent for the decade of the 1960s, but the average real return was −2 percent a year from 1969 through 1974. And the Ibbotson and Sinquefield study showed that the excess of stock over bond rates of return average 5 percentage points *more* for the years after 1951 than for the years before. But historic returns also reflected a shift by many institutions from bonds to stocks, and if this trend slows or is reversed, the gap between bond and stock returns may be expected to narrow.

The compound average real rate of return on treasury bills computed by Ibbotson and Sinquefield was almost zero for 1926–1973. They found the rate to be around 1 percent after 1951, about the time of the Treasury-Federal Reserve accord. It seems reasonable to predict that the real interest rate on treasury bills over the long run will be between 0 and 1 percent. Treasury bills seem to be about the best inflation hedge one can find, because their yields correlate very closely with the rate of inflation, but they simply are not profitable in real terms. This should come as no surprise, since one would expect that the better one is protected from loss due to inflation, the lower the probability that the investment will return any more than the rate of inflation.

REAL RATES OF ENDOWMENT RETURN

Table 3-3 shows predicted long-run average real rates of return for stocks, bonds, treasury bills, and a combination of these, based on historic rates. The combination corresponds approximately to the average for 147 endowment pools for which data were collected as of June 30, 1974.

Since inflation in higher education is probably two to three percentage points above inflation for the economy as a whole, the real return, in terms of higher education purchasing power, of an endowment portfolio is 2 to 3 percentage points lower than what appears in the table.

One question remains with respect to long-run expectations. Can

Table 3-3 Long-Run Predicted Average Real Total Return Rates Based on 1926–73 Results (%)

Stocks	7–8
Bonds	1–3
Treasury bills	0
60% stocks; 30% bonds; 10% treasury bills	4.5–5.5

we not anticipate that good management will not only pay for itself and its transaction costs but also add significantly to the rate of return that a market index might be expected to produce? There is little evidence to support such a hope.

A good deal of research on mutual funds, which are managed by professionals, suggests that on average and over a long period they perform about as well as the market.[24] And formal tests of the ability of mutual fund managers to forecast the stock market suggest that they cannot.[25] With respect to the ability of professionals to forecast interest rates, an ability that might lead to superior rates of return in the bond market, the investment counseling firm of Standish, Ayer and Wood said in its *Bond Bulletin* of February 1975:

> In evaluating the results of the forecast of long-term rates during the twenty quarters [10/2/69 to 7/5/74], it is interesting to note that the experts guessed the direction of rates exactly 50 percent of the time—ten right and ten wrong.

This is not to say that prediction is impossible or that *no* money managers can add to a market rate of return. But it indicates the need for skepticism in forecasting a long-run rate of return for any endowment fund much above the rate of return on the market.

Before the last decade or two, educational endowment funds by and large were conservative in their investment policies. More recently, controversy has arisen over the appropriate level of risk taking. But to appreciate why endowment funds are where they are and why the controversy has arisen, it is necessary to examine briefly the kinds of assets that endowments have favored over the years.

HISTORIC TRENDS

Before the 1830s, almost all college endowment funds were invested in notes, mortgages, advances, and real estate.[1] In the 1830s, substantial investments in common stocks began to appear. (In 1830, the Supreme Court of Massachusetts established the "prudent man" rule.) Following the Civil War, there were substantial issues of government bonds and railroad bonds; during the latter half of the nineteenth century, endowment investment in stocks declined and bond holdings rose. In the 1920s, some endowment funds began to move quite substantially into common stocks, and institutions tended to dispose of real estate and mortgages. During World War II, the accumulation of equities continued, although some endowment funds acquired substantial holdings of government bonds. Investments in mortgages and real estate continued to decline. At the same time, the literature on endowment fund management began to suggest that appreciation, accompanied, of course, by adequate income, was a legitimate investment goal. J. Parker Hall, who was treasurer of the University of Chicago in those years, was one of the most outspoken advocates of investment to produce growing income even at the price of some instability in that income. College and university officials and trustees were beginning to express concern for preserving purchasing power rather than just obtaining the dollar principal of endowment funds.

During the 1950s, endowment portfolios shifted further into equities, and their bond holdings declined. The shift accelerated in the 1960s, with a booming stock market and the introduction of spending techniques that enabled some institutions to convert a portion of stock market profits into expenditure for current uses. Of 31 institutions examined by the author in some detail in 1968, 4 had for many years given considerable emphasis to growth in their investment policies, 7 had made a clear switch from emphasis on income within the preceding five years, 2 had stepped up the emphasis on growth within the preceding year, and 2 were actively discussing a change in investment policy to place greater emphasis on growth. Another 6, although very concerned about the need for emphasis on growth in their investment policies, were moving more slowly.

THE PRESENT-DAY ASSET STRUCTURE

Common stock performance since 1968 has been disappointing, and interest in fixed-income investing has revived. But Cary and Bright were able to report in 1974, as the result of a questionnaire administered in 1972: "Forty percent of the [214] responding educational institutions . . . now include proportionately more growth stocks in their portfolios than they did three years ago."[2]

As of June 30, 1974, the average portfolio of the 147 endowment pools for which questionnaires were returned in the annual NACUBO survey was composed of 60 percent equities, 22 percent senior fixed-income securities, 13 percent treasury bills or other money market instruments, and 5 percent miscellaneous assets. Figure 4-1 shows the variation in the equity proportion of assets.

It appears that during the fiscal year ending June 30, 1974, there was a deliberate shift from equities to fixed-income securities. The average portfolio of these same pools as of June 30, 1973, contained 66 percent equities, 21 percent bonds, 9 percent money market instruments, and 4 percent miscellaneous. If endowment equities suffered the 17.5 percent decline experienced by the Standard & Poor's 500 Index, if bonds suffered the 14.1 percent decline of the Salomon Brothers High-Grade Long-Term Bond Index, and if money market and miscellaneous assets neither appreciated nor declined, then, in the absence of any shifting of assets, the average portfolio as of June 30, 1974, would have contained 64 percent equities, 21 percent

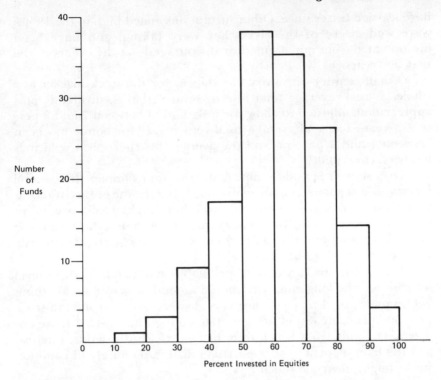

Source: NACUBO survey, June 30, 1974.

Figure 4-1. 147 Pooled Endowment Funds, Percent Investment in Equities, June 30, 1974

bonds, 10 percent money market instruments, and 5 percent miscellaneous. A comparison of these proportions to the actual proportions suggests a deliberate shift of about 3 percent from equities to money market instruments and another 1 percent to bonds. It is hard to tell whether this shift represented a generally more conservative approach or simply a move in anticipation of a declining stock market and opportunities to purchase equities cheaply.

RISK AND RETURN: STOCKS, BONDS, AND TREASURY BILLS

The basic principle of all investment management is that safe investments are rarely very profitable and that aiming at high returns entails high risks. In the late 1960s, a number of institutions forgot this principle or became convinced that it was no longer valid. They have learned better since. Other institutions aimed high in the 1960s, were well aware of the risks they were taking, and have been disappointed—but not alarmed or discouraged—at the events of the past few years.

A half-century of history has shown, for the stock market as a whole, a "real" average total rate of return (that is, dividends plus appreciation, adjusted to allow for inflation) of between 7 and 8 percent a year. The real average total return rate for bonds has been between 1 and 3 percent, and the average for short-term securities has been close to 0.[3]

Over shorter periods of time (a decade, for example), this general relationship is not necessarily maintained. In fact, the events of recent years have led many to wonder whether stocks really are more profitable than bonds. But these events simply counterbalance those of the late 1950s and the early 1960s, when stocks were enormously more profitable than bonds.[4]

If common stocks are more profitable than bonds or short-term securities in the long run, why should an endowment hold anything but common stocks? There are two answers. An all–common-stock portfolio probably would not generate enough income for those endowment funds from which only income yield (dividends, interest, and the like) is spent. And a portfolio made up entirely of common stocks might incur too much risk.

Most observers would agree that a portfolio of common stocks is more risky than a portfolio of bonds (assuming both stocks and bonds to be of reasonably high quality). But they might disagree on how much more risk there is in the stock portfolio and how to measure the risk. Figure 4-2 shows the relationship between average rate of return and variability, one important measure of risk, measured by standard deviation of annual rates of return, for stocks, bonds, and treasury bills over the years 1926–73.

An endowment fund portfolio that consists of both bonds and stocks can certainly be expected to produce a more stable performance from year to year than an all-stock portfolio. If it also includes short-term investments, it will be even more stable. Although long-term bonds may reflect very little risk of default, their market value changes as interest rates change, which may or may not be a matter of concern to trustees. Short-term investments, less sensitive to interest rate changes, can meet liquidity needs and provide a temporary vehicle for funds to be committed to equities when prices are favorable (see Appendix 4).

But, granted that all three kinds of securities have a place in

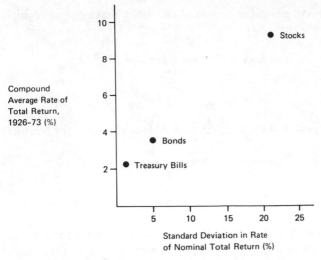

Source: Roger G. Ibbotson and Rex A. Sinquefield, "Stocks, Bonds, Bills, and Inflation: The Past and the Future." Paper presented at the Seminar on the Analysis of Security Prices, Center for Research in Security Prices, Graduate School of Business, University of Chicago, May and November 1974.

Figure 4-2. Variability and Return, 1926-73

endowment funds, how should the proportions of the three be set, and should they be set once for all time or varied to meet changing conditions and expectations? Only in the context of the endowment's place in the overall financial plan for the institution is it possible to arrive at a reasonable balance among rate of return, stability of return, and liquidity. It may be useful, though, to look briefly at the results of some different proportions in good and bad markets.

Consider three strategies. The first is quite aggressive: 85 percent common stocks, 10 percent bonds, and 5 percent short-term securities. The second is more stable: 65 percent common stocks, 30 percent bonds, and 5 percent short-term. And the third is quite conservative: 40 percent common stocks, 50 percent bonds, and 10 percent short-term. Over the 1973–74 period, when the stock market performed extraordinarily badly in terms of compound average total return (not adjusted for inflation), these three strategies performed as follows:[5]

Strategy	Percent per year
1	−17.0
2	−12.9
3	− 7.5

Over 1971–72, a good period in terms of the stock market, the results were

Strategy	Percent per year
1	15.3
2	13.8
3	11.7

Finally, over the period 1926–74, almost half a century, the results were

Strategy	Percent per year
1	7.6
2	6.6
3	5.3

It is easy to see that strategy 3, with the lowest rate of return in periods of a rising stock market (and probably over the long run), produced the smallest fluctuation through good and bad markets. It may be possible to deduce from these examples a rough estimate of what is appropriate for a particular institution. But a careful analysis really demands some simulations, so that one can see the effects of different proportions of stocks, bonds, and short-term securities on portfolio performance.[6]

These three securities categories are not themselves homogeneous, of course. Bonds can be further classified by industry, quality rating, maturity, coupon, call feature, and so on. And these classifications are important in establishing credit risk. The classification of common stocks is more difficult and controversial. An investment committee may want to make the allocation of funds among these subgroups part of the investment policy. Or it may prefer to leave such allocation to the professional manager.

THE ROLE OF MANAGEMENT AND "EFFICIENT" MARKETS

The discussion so far has been in terms of market averages, but is it not the function of a professional money manager to do better than the averages, to achieve a higher rate of return? But a very substantial body of literature, based on research, supports the proposition that most securities markets are rather efficient, in the sense that the prices of all securities correctly reflect all that is known and knowable about those securities, and that therefore no one can systematically do better than the market. One can aim at high returns only by buying high-risk securities, but one cannot expect to achieve any higher return than is consistent with the risk.[7] Not everyone accepts the proposition that the securities markets are efficient, but the record of professional investment management does not provide much basis for expecting managers to deliver more than a "market" rate of return.

But some markets may indeed be more efficient than others, and some markets may even be fairly inefficient. The bond market has traditionally been less efficient than the stock market and has offered greater opportunity to achieve higher rates of return than could be explained by risk. And some components of the stock market appear to be more efficient than others.

Professional managers have always been expected to do better than the market averages by using skill in the selection of securities—buying the undervalued and selling the overvalued. The evidence indicates that investment managers as a group have not established a record of success at selection. Another activity—market timing—has become the focus of particular interest in 1974 and 1975.

Clearly, anyone who in early 1973 could have foreseen the 42 percent decline in the stock market over the next two years could have profited substantially from shifting swiftly from stocks to treasury bills. A manager who had had the foresight to be aggressive (strategy 1 described above) in 1971–72 and conservative (strategy 3) in 1973–74 would have achieved a four-year average total return of 3.3 percent per year. But one who guessed exactly wrong and was aggressive in the down market and conservative in the up market would have produced an average total return of −3.7 percent per year for the four years.

Although some managers were successful in shifting to short-term investments in the 1973–74 period and reducing losses, it is not clear that their success was due to their skill rather than to luck. And if it was the result of skill, this specific skill is not necessarily the one that future years will demand. "Timing" tends to be popular following any dramatic market move because, inevitably, a few managers will be lucky enough to make just the right shifts.

Some research at Stanford University has concluded that freedom to move back and forth between 100 percent short-term securities and 100 percent common stocks, coupled with *perfect* ability to forecast the market, can be expected to add only about 4 percent a year in the long run to what the all–common-stock portfolio would earn. And unless the manager is correct about 75 percent of the time, he will do worse by shifting back and forth than he will by staying with common stocks.[8]

But even if markets are efficient and managers can add little or nothing to market rates of return, management still has an important role. Meeting and, indeed, helping to establish investment objectives, achieving diversification, and even keeping up with market rates of return are significant accomplishments. (For the institution that seeks only these benefits of management and would prefer not to pay the higher fees and incur the greater transactions costs that a search for higher rates of return would involve, some money management firms, for example, Batterymarch Financial Management Corporation of Boston, guarantee the market rate of return.)

INFLATION AND THE CHOICE OF ASSETS

Until recently, the conventional wisdom in the investment world held that common stocks were a hedge against inflation. And then, with the sharp decline in stock prices in 1973 and 1974, the probable decline in dividends for 1975, and extraordinary rates of inflation, many investors began to believe that the old wisdom was no longer valid. It is worth giving some thought to this issue, because it has a great deal to do with investment policy for the years ahead.

A "hedge" is a form of insurance. An investment that is a genuine inflation hedge produces a high rate of return when inflation is high, a modest rate of return when inflation is modest, and a low rate of return when inflation is low. A perfect inflation hedge would be an investment that produced a steady rate of return in terms of purchasing power: a constant real rate of return.

The theoretical argument for common stocks as an inflation hedge runs that if business corporations are able to pass on higher costs in the form of higher prices, they can maintain and increase their earnings and dividends as inflation increases. And if competition brings prices down as costs decline, then earnings and dividends also will fall. But at least in the short run, this theory does not work. One study of three periods of inflation since 1949 (1950–51, 1956–57, and 1966–73) gives "no support for the hypothesis that common stocks are consistent or complete inflation hedges."[9] Another study provides evidence that, over the long run, common stocks suffer when inflation rises and benefit when inflation declines, but that so long as inflation remains constant, even at a high level, real returns on common stocks remain level.[10] In short, common stocks apparently run the same sort of inflation risk as bonds do, but to a lesser degree.

Research conducted at the Federal Reserve Bank of St. Louis indicates that interest rates on long-term bonds are fairly closely related to long-term trends in inflation, while interest rates on short-term fixed-income investments are fairly closely related to short-term inflation.[11] As a matter of fact, treasury bills are the best true inflation hedge. The rate on treasury bills moves quite closely with the rate of inflation, even in the short run. Unfortunately, the real return on treasury bills is close to zero.

The research in this area leads to the conclusion that in times of rapid inflation, common stocks will probably perform badly. But even if common stocks are a poor inflation hedge, they will almost certainly prove more profitable in the long run than will fixed-income investments, because they produce a higher real rate of return.

BEYOND STOCKS AND BONDS

In considering the alternatives to stocks, bonds, and money market instruments as investment media for endowment funds, it may be well to establish first what they may have to offer that stocks and bonds do not. For example, they may offer the prospect of greater return for the same risk, perhaps as the result of some imperfection in the marketplace. For example, if investors generally did not realize that the options market offered greater rates of return for the same risk than could be obtained in the stock market, then those investors who knew better might do well. Such an advantage is unlikely to last, but it may sometimes be found in relatively new investment markets. Another reason for expecting returns beyond those justified by risk may be the existence of disadvantages other than risk of loss associated with an investment. Relatively high rates of return may compensate for the lack of liquidity in mortgages, for example, or in real estate ownership. Many endowment funds may find that liquidity is not a pressing need and that it can be sacrificed readily for higher returns. Certain other investments that offer relatively high returns may also present management problems that are as much a deterrent to endowment funds as to anyone else. Both mortgages and real estate equities call for special management expertise that most colleges and universities do not possess. And both present considerable difficulties in achieving diversification.

Another possibility is that, although an investment medium does not offer generally higher rates of return for the same risk, it offers greater scope for investment expertise because its market is less efficient. The bond market, for example, may be less efficient that the stock market. Real estate equities and the call option market also may be less efficient and may offer opportunities for unusually good returns (see Appendixes 6 and 7). Security lending is another device that offers the chance for enhanced returns (see Appendix 5).

Finally, even an investment medium that does not offer the prospect of greater returns for the same level of risk that can be found in the stock and bond markets may offer new opportunities for diversification. For example, although real estate equities may be no more profitable than common stocks, they may offer diversification. When stocks are down, real estate equities may be doing well, and when real estate is down, stocks may be up. Call option writing offers even more distinctive opportunities since the very purpose of writing call options is to hedge against losses on common stocks.

A number of institutions invest endowment funds in their own physical plant; others have been hesitant about using true endowments for this purpose. Certainly, an excessive reliance on endowment to finance plant assets can lead to an inability to repay the endowment and can convert an earning asset into a nonearning asset. Perhaps policy should restrict the plant investments of endowment funds to revenue-producing plants, such as dormitories and dining halls, with user fees that can service the advance from the endowment. The institution may not necessarily find it easier to repay advances for revenue-producing plants than advances for other physical facilities. But the restriction may still serve to keep the magnitude of these advances at a reasonable level. At most institutions, advances for physical plants are repaid with interest at a full market rate.

In recent years, institutions have been presented with opportunities to invest in student loans, many of which can be insured by the federal government or by state agencies. The warehousing and purchase programs of the Student Loan Marketing Association (by which institutions can borrow money, using student notes as collateral, and can sell student notes outright) offer some liquidity to a student loan portfolio. Apart from these programs, institutions are not likely to find an easy way to dispose of loans before they are paid off. This should not constitute a serious difficulty, unless student loans make up an excessive portion of endowment investments.

RISK AND THE "PRUDENT MAN" RULE

All of these investment media have risks: some are inherent in the media themselves and others are a function of the institution's management capability and of the overall diversification among assets and among kinds of assets.

Cary and Bright observe that the investment standards for trustees in most states are those set out in the classic prudent man rule.[12] This rule, as first enunciated in 1830, requires trustees to

> exercise the judgment and care under the circumstances then prevailing which men of prudence, discretion and intelligence exercise in the management of their own affairs, not in regard to speculation, but in regard to the permanent disposition of their funds, considering the probable income as well as the probable safety of their capital.[13]

Section 6 of the model Uniform Management of Institutional Funds Act modifies this rule somewhat, making it closer to the standard generally required of the director of a business corporation:

> SECTION 6. [*Standard of Conduct.*] In the administration of the powers to appropriate appreciation, to make and retain investments, and to delegate investment management of institutional funds, members of a governing board shall exercise ordinary business care and prudence under the facts and circumstances prevailing at the time of the action or decision. In so doing they shall consider long and short term needs of the institution in carrying out its educational, religious, charitable, or other eleemosynary purposes, its present and anticipated financial requirements, expected total return on its investments, price level trends, and general economic conditions.

The prudent man rule was developed long before people began to think in terms of diversified portfolios and the risk and return characteristics of those portfolios. So it was first applied as a test of the propriety of investment in particular securities. But today a portfolio invested exclusively in moderate-risk securities may have overall risk characteristics similar to those of a portfolio invested partly in extremely safe securities and partly in securities of relatively high risk. Hence these two portfolios may be equally appropriate to any particular endowment fund.

But it is not clear whether a trustee must be prepared to justify every security in a portfolio as being a prudent selection or whether it is enough that the portfolio as a whole is prudent. For a time in 1971, it appeared that the issue was going to be resolved by the courts. Hanover College of Indiana sued Donaldson, Lufkin and Jenretté on the grounds that the latter, when acting as investment adviser with discretionary powers, purchased 16 common stocks that were "unseasoned, speculative, volatile and risky," leading to losses of $2.4 million.[14] Hanover College had indeed sought aggressive management. Its president, in a 1968 article in *College and University Business Administration*,[15] said that, in selecting its new investment adviser, the college was seeking substantially above-average investment returns. And he spoke of the outstanding 24 percent increase in the endowment for the year ending June 30, 1968. His trustees had determined to commit 10 percent of the endowment to fixed-income securities and 90 percent to investment in common stocks.

In suing its investment adviser, Hanover College was attempting to apply the prudent man rule on a stock-by-stock basis, challenging individual stocks as unsuitable for inclusion in an endowment fund. Had the case gone to court (it was actually settled out of court), Donaldson, Lufkin would almost certainly have replied that the prudent man test should be applied to the entire portfolio and that the overall risk characteristic of the portfolio was consistent with the needs of the college, at least as expressed by its trustees. The college president's statement did suggest that the overall risk level of the portfolio was rather high and that it reflected the preference of the trustess. The portfolio was extremely volatile, rising 24 percent for the year ending June 30, 1968, when the Standard & Poor's Composite Index rose 14 percent and the Dow Jones Industrial Average rose 7 percent. And the prudence of the overall portfolio strategy was open to question. But it would be unfortunate if the courts were to demand that every security in the portfolio individually qualify under the prudent man rule, as though it were the sole investment of the endowment fund. (The case does raise an interesting question as to the responsibility of a professional investment manager who is asked by an investment committee to follow a possibly imprudent policy.)

One case, decided in late 1974 by the New York Court of Appeals, in fact suggests that the prudent man rule calls for a stock-by-stock scrutiny of a portfolio. In *Matter of Bank of New York*,[16] the guardian ad litem had objected to some investment decisions of the bank trust department in managing its common trust fund. The objections had been dismissed on a motion for summary judgment, and the Court of Appeals upheld the dismissal but made some observations by way of dicta that have created uneasiness among trustees and investment managers. The court quoted a standard of care essentially the same as the Massachusetts prudent man rule but then went on to say:

The fact that this portfolio showed substantial overall increase in total value during the accounting period does not insulate the trustee from responsibility for imprudence with respect to individual investments for which it would otherwise be surcharged . . . to hold to the contrary would in effect be to assure fiduciary immunity in an advancing market such as marked the history of the accounting period here involved. The record of any individual investment is not to be viewed exclusively, of course, as though it were in its own water-tight compartment, since to some extent individual investment decisions may properly be affected by considerations of the performance of the fund as an entity, as in the instance, for example, of individual security decisions based in part on considerations of diversification of the fund or of capital transactions to achieve sound tax planning for the fund as a whole. The focus of inquiry, however, is nonetheless on the individual security as such and factors relating to the entire portfolio are to be weighed only along with others in reviewing the prudence of the particular investment decisions.[17]

The quotation is somewhat ambiguous. It suggests that a trustee must be prepared to defend each security in a portfolio as meeting a prudent man standard, but it offers diversification as an important element to be considered. The author's interpretation is that a trustee need not show that an entire portfolio could be prudently invested in a security in order to justify inclusion of that security in the portfolio, but that some single securities might be regarded as so outlandish that no amount of diversification could justify their purchase.

The prudent man rule itself does not explicitly deal with diversification, but few professional investors would ignore the importance of diversification in reducing risk. The Pension Reform Act of 1974 refers to diversification as an element in prudent management (see Appendix 8). This statute does not, of course, apply to endowment funds, but it may be influential in setting standards and it may be an indication of legislation to come.

The test of prudence in the Pension Reform Act is also of interest because it demands the care and skill of a prudent man "familiar with such matters"—i.e., familiar with investments—and thus goes somewhat beyond the Massachusetts prudent man rule.

A significant innovation in Section 6 of the Uniform Act is the reference to "anticipated financial requirements" and to "price level trends." These considerations are obviously relevant to establishing a spending policy, but they also indicate that trustees are to take into account the risk of lost purchasing power due to inflation in their investment decision making.

CHOOSING THE "MIX" OF INVESTMENTS

An investment committee will wisely refrain from choosing individual securities. That is what professional managers are trained to do, and interfering with their work is not likely to be beneficial. But the setting of policy is the committee's business and should not be left to the manager. And determining policy involves making some decisions with respect to the mix of securities or other assets in which the endowment is to be invested.

It may be useful to ask the professional manager for his estimate of the risk and return for each class of investment and for his judgment as to a suitable mix, partly to see whether he and the committee are in reasonable agreement as to the expectations for each class and partly to see whether he is likely to aim at the overall performance the committee has in mind.

The committee should certainly consider investment media other than stocks, bonds, and money market instruments, obtaining advice where it can and weighing what these investments may have to offer, in risk and return terms, relative to more conventional investments.

Inflation presents a serious risk to a college or university, as important as any other investment risk. A committee cannot afford to neglect this risk in order to attend to the traditional task of simply protecting principal. But no single form of investment has proved completely effective in dealing with inflation.

V/*Spending Policy*

Of all the changes that have affected endowment fund management in the last decade, probably the one that has given rise to the greatest controversy and the deepest soul searching has been the trend toward so-called total-return investing and spending. In the course of a survey conducted some seven years ago, it became clear that the financial officers of about thirty educational institutions believed that one of the two most important aspects of their investment policy was "the relative importance to be given to current yield and to growth or to total return."[1] (The other aspect was the selection of a manager or investment adviser.) Subsequent surveys, speeches, and publications suggest that this concern has not diminished.

There is fairly wide agreement that total return as an investment objective is a good thing. The investment manager is expected to make the endowment fund as profitable as possible, within reasonable risk limitations, without regard for whether the profit takes the form of income yield (dividends, interest, and the like) or appreciation in market value. A total-return investment policy leaves the manager free to decide whether an emphasis on income yield or an emphasis on growth or a combination of the two is likely to be most profitable at any particular time. There is evidence that high-yield securities generally produce lower total returns than low-yield securities do. (Appreciation may not appear to be of direct use to an institution, but it is certainly of indirect benefit since it facilitates an increase in income.)

But the traditional practice of educational and charitable institutions has been to spend only income yield on true endowment funds, treating appreciation, whether realized or unrealized, as a part of principal and therefore unexpendable. "True endowment" funds are those for which there is a legal obligation to preserve principal. (For endowment funds that do not carry this restriction, so-called quasi-

endowment funds, or "funds functioning as endowment," the trustees
of an institution are legally free to invade principal and may therefore
spend income and realized or unrealized gains at their discretion.) A
number of institutions have had difficulty in reconciling the traditional spending rule for true endowment with a total-return investment policy. As a result, some new approaches to spending policy
have emerged.

TRADITIONAL INVESTMENT AND SPENDING POLICIES

The word "endowment" has been defined, in what Cary and
Bright describe as "the landmark decision in the field," as "the be-
stowment of money as a permanent fund, the income of which is to be
used in the administration of a proposed work."[2] And one can find in
the Oxford English dictionary quotations that illustrate this use of the
word dating from the fifteenth or sixteenth century. In fact, this sort
of endowment dates back at least to the twelfth century, when substantial quantities of land were dedicated to the perpetual support of
religious organizations.

In those early days, the distinction between "income," available
for the support of the institution, and "principal," to be held in per-
petuity, was probably quite clear. Income would have included the
fruits of the land, one of which might be rent. Over time, land values
and rents tended to rise, and the increase in rental income not only
enabled the endowed institutions to cope with inflation but also provided for expanded activities and a somewhat higher standard of
living.

During the early history of charitable endowments, the law of
trusts developed the distinction between income and principal, treating appreciation in the value of the principal as a part of principal
rather than as income. The charitable organizations, although not
strictly governed by the law of trusts, appear to have found this distinction one they could comfortably live with, and for some centuries
it apparently worked very well.

In the early years of the United States, substantial land holdings
apparently formed a source of endowment income for many educational institutions. But by the early twentieth century, the bulk of
educational endowment assets appears to have been invested chiefly
in fixed-income securities, largely bonds and mortgages. This shift
probably reflected the increasing availability of these securities as well
as a growing conservatism on the part of those responsible for invest-

ment. It is hard to tell if trustees gave much thought to the sacrifice in potential appreciation of both principal and income that a switch from real estate holdings to fixed-income investments represented. In any case, the traditional spending rule survived the change in investment strategy, and there does not seem to have been any concern that perhaps at least a portion of the interest income on a fixed-income portfolio should be reinvested to provide for a rising income stream.

Preservation of capital seems to have been the watchword of the endowment fund manager during the early years of the twentieth century. And preservation of capital clearly meant the preservation of "book value"—that is, the dollar value of funds when given to the institution—not preservation of purchasing power or "real value." Equity investments are generally despised. According to one source quoted by Cary and Bright, "Fifty years ago most trustees would have argued that it was immoral to purchase common stocks with endowment funds,"[3] although the "prudent man rule" was originally set out in a decision that supported trust investment in common stock.[4]

Before World War II, only a few institutions had begun to recognize the importance of growth investment performance and the need to include some equities in an endowment portfolio. In 1936, Stanford University went to court in California to obtain explicit authority to purchase equities for an endowment that for its first 51 years had invested only in fixed-income securities. Following World War II, attitudes at many institutions changed.

THE PRESSURE FOR CHANGE

In the 1950s and 1960s, the costs of educational institutions were rising rapidly, in part because of general inflation but more because of the widespread broadening of programs, substantial efforts to improve the quality of education, and a general catching up in salary levels. As a result, educational institutions began making increased demands on their endowments for spendable funds. At the same time, the stock market was performing extraordinarily well and mutual funds were reporting astounding rates of appreciation. It became increasingly difficult to argue against the participation of educational institutions in these gains.

In 1966, his first year as president of the Ford Foundation, McGeorge Bundy chided educational institutions for the conservatism apparent in their endowment portfolios. In 1969, the Barker Report, *Managing Educational Endowments*,[5] also urged a more aggressive stance. Trustees who were dissatisfied with the record of the past used both of these commentaries to persuade their colleagues to turn investment strategy toward more equities.

But shifting from a fixed-income portfolio to a portfolio strong in equities, particularly in growth stocks, generally reduced the level of income yield (that is, interest and dividends). So institutions that made this shift faced an immediate reduction in the contribution of the endowment to the support of current operations.

Some endowed institutions were able to make do with a modest income. Others spent the principal of quasi-endowment funds or used reserves or made a special effort to attract gifts to "bridge the trough" in income. The institutions that were able to do this were generally rewarded with a rapidly rising level of income. Other institutions were not so fortunate. Those that could not sustain even a temporary decline in spendable income either stayed with high-yielding fixed-income investments or perhaps ventured into high-yielding but low-growth equities. The traditional spending rule, coupled with an urgent need for current spending, simply precluded their enjoyment of the benefits of a booming stock market.

Not surprisingly, the spending rule was challenged. Specifically, it was proposed that it would be proper for endowed educational institutions to spend, in addition to income yield, a portion of the appreciation in the value of the endowment fund principal.

The notion of spending appreciation was actually only one aspect of the more general proposal that regardless of the income yield or appreciation in any particular year, the spending in that year should be appropriate to the long-run earning potential of the endowment and the long-run needs of the institution. But the most obvious and controversial aspect of this policy was the likelihood of spending more than income yield.

THE MORAL ISSUE

The traditional spending rule was defended on the grounds that the donors of the original endowment funds had anticipated that the trustees would follow this rule and that to break it would constitute betrayal of their trust. But as Cary and Bright point out, quoting Austin Scott, it is hard to know just what the original donors would have said about the expenditure of a portion of appreciation.[6] The traditional spending rule offers no guarantee that there will be any appreciation at all. A policy of investing in fixed-income securities and preserving principal virtually guarantees that there will be no appreciation. If an institution sacrifices income yield and invests in such a way as to produce some appreciation, is it betraying its donors if it spends a portion of that appreciation?

A more common argument in favor of the traditional rule antici-pated that the spending of some appreciation would soon lead to the spending of *all* appreciation, with growth of the endowment fund and its contribution to institutional budgets being eliminated. This argument was probably heard most strongly from the institutions that had recognized the need for growth and had shifted their investments into equities while continuing to live on the income yield. Harvard was an outstanding example of this class of institution, and from Harvard came some of the strongest language supporting the moral propriety of the traditional spending rule.[7]

The answer to this argument was probably best expressed at Yale. The Yale Treasurer's Report for 1965–66 included these passages:

> In the past we have not had a satisfactory means of judging whether a decision to spend for Operating Expenses a portion of Endowment Funds above Yield was prudent as a desirable sup-port of present needs, or imprudent as a reduction of funds which should be saved to provide for the future. The rule-of-thumb followed was to try to spend only the Yield for Operating Expenses.
>
> Concerning this two points should be made. First, it is only by coincidence that Yield will be a correct balance between the present and the future. Some institutions in their particular cir-cumstances ought to save some Yield; others in theirs ought to spend something beyond Yield. Second, when Yield is the sole measure of what be spent for present needs, a situation of annually increasing needs, such as has obtained for many years and seems likely to continue for many more, forces investment policy to seek to improve current Yield. But this, in turn, under market conditions prevailing most of the time since World War II, could only be done at the expense of a loss of some potential Gain. Many common stocks, both sound and attractive from an institutional point of view, have offered good Yield and a reason-able prospect of growth of Yield, and a Gain as well. However, others, also sound and attractive but affording greater annual Returns in Yield plus Gain, have paid at the outset a relatively low rate of Yield on the initial investment, while producing over time both an increased rate of Yield on the initial investment, and good Gain.
>
> In these circumstances over-stressing of current Yield in choosing common stocks conflicts with the general position of professional portfolio managers who seek the best performance. They hold, as is well known, that a dollar of Yield should not be

considered any better than a dollar of Gain, and that the best over-all Returns (Yield plus Gain) have been obtained when the portfolio manager is free to achieve a Return in whatever Ratio of Yield and Gain is best suited to available market opportunities within the general investment policies appropriate for the particular portfolio owner.

. . .

It is a paradox of Yale's current financial situation that the Yield of the present portfolio would balance present budgets, even at percentage rates of Return below those now afforded by high-grade corporate bonds, if there were a relatively high proportion of fixed income investments and high-yield but lower Gain common stocks. But then Gain would be retarded, Return would be lower, and the future would be prejudiced.

On the other hand, if the proportion of selected common stocks of better growth is increased, although Return (and in time Yield, too) is higher, and the future is better provided for, under recent economic conditions current Yield declines, and service to the present is prejudiced if expenditure must be confined to Yield.[8]

The Yale treasurer's statement points to the need for the trustees of an institution to make an explicit decision with respect to spending from an endowment. They must decide how much it is appropriate to spend to meet the current needs of their institution and how much should be saved to support spending in the future. The result may be spending that is greater or less than income yield. The institution that simply follows the traditional rule of spending whatever comes in the form of income yield is letting its investment policy dictate the choice between spending now and spending later. And as Yale's treasurer points out, an investment strategy that is successful at making money is not necessarily a satisfactory guide to the allocation of resources between present and future.

Arriving at an explicit spending policy is not easy, and some trustees probably would prefer to avoid this task. But clearly, trustees must be responsible for allocating resources and achieving a fair and reasonable balance of spending over time to meet the needs of their particular institutions. The institution hovering on the brink of bankruptcy is hardly in a position to save for the future. And even an institution in tolerable financial condition may need substantial spending *now* to build its academic strength to cope with increasing competition for students or faculty. On the other hand, an institution that anticipates the undertaking of substantial new programs or the loss of substantial revenue sources in future years may find it quite appropriate to hold down current spending from endowment in order to prepare for heavier spending in future years. Many institutions favor a position of "neutrality" between present and future spending which calls for a steady level of real spending, which means a level of dollar spending rising just fast enough to keep up with the institution's own rate of inflation.

The moral issue remains, but supporters of the traditional rule appear to be in a minority. In 1971, when Louis Harris and Associates surveyed 214 colleges and universities, 70 percent of the respondents approved treating part of capital gains on endowment as spendable income. Ten percent of the respondents disapproved somewhat of this practice, and another 14 percent strongly disapproved. Forty-six percent of the respondents indicated that their institutions were already aiming at maximizing total return rather than maximizing current income. Another 10 percent expected to move to this objective. Only 20 percent either had considered the objective and rejected it or had decided not even to consider it.[9] Responses to the NACUBO questionnaire of June 30, 1974, indicated, however, that of 147 pooled endowment funds only 57 had a total-return investment objective and 90 were income-oriented.

THE LEGAL ARGUMENT

We have seen endowment defined as a fund from which the income is to be used for the support of an institution. The legal debate about spending has generally focused on the meaning of the term "income." Until around the mid-1960s, almost all legal opinions on this question concluded that income could not include appreciation. But in 1969, Cary and Bright reported that they could find no court decision on the question as it applied to charitable endowment funds.[10] The law of private trusts clearly attributed appreciation to principal rather than to income, and the legal force of the traditional spending rule for endowment funds had to rest on an analogy to the private trust. Cary and Bright argued that the analogy was inappropriate. The reason for separating principal and income in the case of the private trust generally involves the proper allocation of property between income beneficiaries and "remainderman." (The "remainderman" of a trust is entitled to the assets of the trust at the end of the period during which the income beneficiary is entitled to the income.) But in the case of the charitable or educational endowment fund, the

institution is at the same time both income beneficiary and remainderman.[11] The distinction between principal and income serves only
to bring about a proper allocation between spending in the present
and spending in the future. The allocation of appreciation either to
principal or to income in this case is somewhat arbitrary, and the
trustees of an institution can effectively defeat any legal restrictions
on allocation by means of an investment strategy that produces income but no appreciation, appreciation but no income, or some combination of the two.

Cary and Bright concluded that the definition of income used for
business corporations was a more appropriate guide for educational
endowments than was the definition of income used for private trusts.
And the definition of income of a business corporation includes
realized, although not necessarily unrealized, appreciation. The distinction between realized and unrealized appreciation for a charitable
endowment seems illogical, since the latter can be converted into the
former at any time upon payment of transaction expenses. But although they felt that a court might be expected to rely on the analogy
to the business corporation and to permit the spending of realized
appreciation as income, Cary and Bright were not confident that the
courts would go so far as to permit the spending of unrealized appreciation.

Cary and Bright's monograph, published in 1969, contains a
carefully thought out legal rationale for a new spending policy. The
authors felt that, in order to be defensible, a policy permitting the
expenditure of appreciation had to have some standards of prudence
built into it. And they proposed a kind of prudent man standard,
calling for the addition to principal of enough realized appreciation to
offset inflation and bring about a steady level of real spendable income.[12]

Even before the publication of the Cary and Bright report, some
institutions had reached the same conclusions and had begun to treat
a portion of appreciation on endowment funds as available for current spending. Some institutions avoided the legal issue by retaining
the traditional spending rule for true endowment funds and turning
to the new rule only for quasi-endowment funds, from which they
were legally entitled to spend whatever they wished. In 1965, Yale
University conducted a review of the gift instruments relating to all of
the funds in its endowment, sorted these funds into true endowment
and quasi endowment, and turned to the new spending approach for
its quasi-endowment funds. But in succeeding years, other institutions
followed the Cary and Bright logic all the way, applying the new
spending rule to all endowment funds, both true and quasi.

Dartmouth College and Smith College were among the first to
the move. For a while, the legal justification for this position ha
rest almost entirely on the logic that Cary and Bright had followed i
their report. But there was soon legislative support for the new rule.

NEW LEGISLATION

The most important legislation with respect to endowment fund
spending is the Uniform Management of Institutional Funds Act,
which was very much influenced by the reasoning of Cary and Bright.
The Act was approved by the Conference of Commissioners on Uniform State Laws in 1972 and has served as the pattern for legislation
in 16 states (the 16 statutes are not identical and reflect various mod-
ifications of the pattern): California, Colorado, Connecticut, Delaware, Illinois, Kansas, Maine, Maryland, Minnesota, Montana, New
Hampshire, North Dakota, Tennessee, Vermont, Virginia, and
Washington.[13]
The Act permits the spending of a portion of appreciation on
endowment funds, but it does not do this by incorporating appreciation in the definition of income. It simply authorizes the spending of a
prudent portion of appreciation in addition to what is ordinarily defined as income. This avoids all of the accounting complications that
would follow from tampering with the definition of income. The Act
draws no distinction between realized and unrealized appreciation:
both are available for spending. Section 2 of the Act reads:

> SECTION 2. [*Appropriation of Appreciation.*] The governing board
> may appropriate for expenditure for the uses and purposes for
> which an endowment fund is established so much of the net
> appreciation, realized and unrealized, in the fair value of the
> assets of an endowment fund over the historic dollar value of the
> fund as is prudent under the standard established by Section 6.
> This Section does not limit the authority of the governing board
> to expend funds as permitted under other law, the terms of the
> applicable gift instrument, or the charter of the institution.

The reference to "historic dollar value" is important. The Act reads:
> . . . "historic dollar value" means the aggregate fair value in dol-
> lars of (i) an endowment fund at the time it became an endow-
> ment fund, (ii) each subsequent donation to the fund at the time
> it is made, and (iii) each accumulation made pursuant to a direc-
> tion in the applicable gift instrument at the time the accumulation
> is added to the fund. The determination of historic dollar value
> made in good faith by the institution is conclusive.

The amount of appreciation that may be spent in a particular fiscal year is a function not of the appreciation or depreciation of that particular year but of the cumulative appreciation of the fund over its historic dollar value. An endowment fund that is heavily invested in equities may find that its historic dollar value is close to current market value at the end of a long decline in the stock market, particularly if a large portion of the endowment is made up of gifts recently received. Once market value declines to historic dollar value, Section 2 of the Uniform Act permits no further spending of appreciation and limits spending to income yield. A number of institutions have encountered this situation in recent years. (Needless to say, very careful record keeping is necessary in periods of market decline to assure compliance with Section 2.)

Only a prudent portion of appreciation is eligible for spending. Section 6 of the Act deals with the standard of prudence:

> SECTION 6. [*Standard of Conduct.*] In the administration of the powers to appropriate appreciation, to make and retain investments, and to delegate investment management of institutional funds, members of a governing board shall exercise ordinary business care and prudence under the facts and circumstances prevailing at the time of the action or decision. In so doing they shall consider long and short term needs of the institution in carrying out its educational, religious, charitable, or other eleemosynary purposes, its present and anticipated financial requirements, expected total return on its investments, price level trends, and general economic conditions.

This is essentially the standard suggested by Cary and Bright.

The Uniform Act authorizes the spending of a prudent portion of appreciation even for those funds that were given to the institution on the specific terms that spending was to be limited to income or that principal was to be maintained intact. But Section 3 of the Act permits the donor to preserve the traditional spending rule for his gift, if this is what he wants:[14]

> SECTION 3. [*Rule of Construction.*] Section 2 does not apply if the applicable gift instrument indicates the donor's intention that net appreciation shall not be expended. A restriction upon the expenditure of net appreciation may not be implied from a designation of a gift as an endowment, or from a direction or authorization in the applicable gift instrument to use only "income," "interest," "dividends," or "rents, issues or profits," or "to preserve the principal intact," or a direction which contains other words of

similar import. This rule of construction applies to gift instruments executed or in effect before or after the effective date of this Act.

In a sense, this section creates a new class of true endowment.

A few states that have not passed statutes based on the Uniform Act have adopted substantially similar legislation.[15] The New York State Not-for-Profit Corporation Law was amended in 1973 to apply to educational institutions and provides that income from an endowment fund may include a prudent portion of *realized* appreciation of principal, provided that the market value of the remaining principal is no less than the value of the assets when they were originally given to the institution (the historic dollar value limitation). Pennsylvania has a substantially similar provision in its Non-Profit Corporation Law, but instead of insisting on the preservation of the historic dollar value of gifts, Pennsylvania limits the allocation of realized gains to income to 9 percent of the value of the assets remaining after the allocation. North Carolina leaves it to the trustees of the constituent institutions of the University of North Carolina to determine what is income and what is principal with respect to their endowment funds. And the New Jersey Educational Endowment Management Act permits educational institutions, with the approval of the New Jersey Superior Court, to adopt a plan for allocating to current operating expenses endowment pool income "in excess of the actual interest, dividends, income, rates, issues and profits yielded or earned by the endowment pool."

A 1972 survey of educational institutions in the United States by Cary and Bright found that 62 percent of the institutions responding believed that it was legal to spend capital gains from true endowment funds and 25 percent of these institutions had changed their opinions on this legal point within the preceding three years.[16] Of 136 institutions responding the NACUBO survey of June 30, 1974, 40 reported spending policies making use of yield and gains on true endowment funds, 9 spent yield and gains only on quasi endowment, and 87 spent only income yield.

PRACTICAL ASPECTS OF A CHANGED SPENDING RULE

The shift from the traditional spending rule to a policy of spending at least a portion of appreciation on endowment funds came about in a context of booming equity markets. During the 1960s, educational endowment funds also began to emphasize growth and heavier investment in common stocks. Some institutions, those able to live on a modest income yield, shifted into common stocks with low yield and high growth prospects some years before they embarked upon the spending of appreciation. Other institutions were able to make the shift into growth-oriented investments only because of the new spending rule.

There is a certain irony in the fact that, in at least one respect, the traditional spending rule works better than the new spending rule for an endowment that is heavily invested in equities. The emphasis on equities tends to increase the fluctuation in market value of the endowment fund. The traditional spending rule may still lead to relatively stable spending from year to year, because the flow of dividends will be relatively stable despite the fluctuations in stock prices, unless there are significant moves among high- and low-dividend stocks or between stocks and fixed-income investments. But the new spending rule may lead to substantial variation in spending as the market value of the endowment fluctuates. Most of the institutions shifting to the new rule anticipated a problem in stabilizing their spending, but few were prepared to deal adequately with the very wide fluctuations shown by the stock market in the past few years.

Adoption of the new spending rule, whether only for quasi-endowment funds or for all endowment funds, generally requires the use of a formula linking spending from endowment to the market value of the endowment. The formula must first strike an appropriate balance between current and future spending. This involves the choice of a spending rate. Beyond this, the formula also must serve two conflicting objectives: maximum stability or, even better, a stable growth rate in spending from year to year; and maximum assurance that spending in any year is reasonably consistent with the actual investment performance of the endowment fund. For example, suppose an institutional endowment fund has a current market value of $10 million. The trustees estimate a future average rate of total return of 12 percent a year. They estimate that the institution will experience a rate of inflation in costs of about 7 percent a year, so they conclude that it will be appropriate to spend 5 percent. They plan to begin by spending 5 percent of $10 million, or $500,000. They anticipate growth of 7 percent, so they anticipate spending $535,000 a year later, and they expect that the fund will grow by 7 percent to $10,700,000. The spending-stability objective would be ideally served by a rule that says, spend $500,000 during the coming year and increase the spending by 7 percent in each succeeding year. But suppose the endowment fund does not achieve a total rate of return of 12 percent. If the actual rate turns out to be less than this amount, then the projected spending may be regarded as excessive. The trustees can meet the objective of consistency with actual returns by waiting until the end of the year to learn the actual total-return rate achieved by the endowment fund and then spending a prudent portion of that total return. But this strategy will produce substantial fluctuations in year-to-year spending as well as extraordinary obstacles to budgeting, at least if the endowment is invested in equities whose prices fluctuate.

One must somehow reach a compromise between intolerable fluctuation in spending and intolerable risk that spending may seriously outrun investment performance. When trustees were first developing spending formulas to cope with the new spending rule, they tended to emphasize the second objective. This is not surprising, considering that they were embarking on an untried spending strategy the legality of which, in many cases, was not entirely certain. The result was spending formulas that led, in the late 1960s and early 1970s, to budgeted spending from endowments which institutions simply could not live with. Few institutions had difficulty raising their spending to make use of the large budgeted spending resulting from a very successful investment performance. But years of poor performance, of which there were altogether too many in the late 1960s and early 1970s, led to budget reductions that the institutions could not endure. As a result, trustees were forced to spend more from endowment than their spending formulas called for. Whether or not this extra spending represented a "deficit" (institutions used a variety of terms for it), the spending formulas clearly were not working adequately. They created the illusion of a strict discipline on spending from endowment. But once institutions conceded that the spending formula could not be followed, in many cases they had no other discipline to fall back on. One college president discovered that, on the one hand, he simply could not live with the formula and therefore had to appeal to his trustees for permission to spend more from the endowment fund than the formula permitted and, on the other hand, he was unable to provide his staff with firm guidelines as to the level of spending that would ultimately be permitted.

There were further difficulties. The Uniform Act requires that the spending of appreciation not bring the market value of true endowment below its historic cost. For these funds then, the institutions could not spend more than income yield. In order to sustain the planned spending rate for the entire endowment fund, they had to spend at a somewhat higher rate from funds whose market value was still above historic cost or, more likely, from quasi-endowment funds on which there was no legal limitation on spending. (Another solution lay in emphasizing high-yield investments.) Institutions that established an overall level of spending consistent with the application of the new spending rule to all endowment funds, charging true endowment funds only with income yield and taking all of the appreciation spending out of quasi-endowment funds, encountered a similar problem. In both cases, as securities markets declined, the quasi-endowment funds bore a very heavy burden, and some institutions could foresee the possibility of those funds being exhausted.

These problems gave rise to a variety of new spending rules and to some serious efforts to arrive at solutions through careful analysis and research. In 1973 and 1974, The Common Fund commissioned studies of yield and gain spending rules. The second study will be published in 1975[17] and is the source of most of the material in the balance of the present chapter.

DEVELOPMENT OF A SPENDING POLICY

For purposes of establishing a policy, it is important to distinguish between income on an endowment and appropriate spending from the endowment. The total productivity of an endowment fund comes in the form of income and appreciation. Appropriate spending is related to the total productivity and not simply to the income or to the appreciation. Some institutions may feel that they are still precluded from spending any more than income yield. But this should not stand in the way of their developing a spending policy and determining what is an appropriate amount to spend. If it turns out that this appropriate amount is less than the income yield, then there is no conflict between appropriate spending and a yield limitation. On the other hand, if it turns out that an appropriate spending level exceeds income yield, the institution will have to decide whether to change its investment strategy in order to increase the yield or whether simply to hold spending below the level that is really appropriate. There may be other ways to deal with the problem, involving stabilization reserves or the use of quasi endowment, but the point is that the development of a spending policy, independent of what the income yield on a fund happens to be, is a trustee responsibility in every college and university.

A critical part of every spending policy is the rate of spending, expressed as a percentage of market value of the endowment fund. The selection of this rate is a significant policy decision.

CHOOSING THE SPENDING RATE

In order to establish a spending rate, what a board of trustees usually does to get the best advice it can with respect to both the probable long-run total rate of return on the endowment fund and the probable rate of inflation in the costs of the institution. The difference between these two rates will be the appropriate spending rate so long as the objective is simply to maintain the purchasing power of the endowment and of endowment spending over the years.[18]

Some institutions may find it appropriate to aim at something other than level purchasing power over the years. In such cases, trustees will have to deal with many more issues in setting their spending rate. At a minimum, they must make fairly careful projections of revenues and expenditures for a 5- to 10-year period in order to deduce the demands they will be making on their endowment.

Harvard University has adopted a policy of maintaining constant purchasing power, and the Harvard Financial Report for June 30, 1974, describes the derivation of Harvard's spending rate. The total return on the endowment fund was estimated at 8 percent, gifts were expected to add another 2 percent of growth, and an overall growth rate of 6 percent seemed necessary to cope with inflation. So 4 percent was left for spending.

The NACUBO survey of June 30, 1974, found that of twenty-five institutions making use of a spending rate applied to the market value of their endowments, two were using 6 percent or more, sixteen were using 5 to 6 percent, and four were using 4 to 5 percent. Some 140 members of The Common Fund withdraw 5 percent of a three-year average of the market value of their investment in the fund, but of course they do not necessarily apply the same spending rule to their entire endowments.

For an endowment fund invested 60 percent in common stocks, 30 percent in bonds, and 10 percent in short-term investments (roughly the average composition of 147 endowment pools as of June 30, 1974), a spending rate somewhere between 4.5 and 5.5 percent will probably enable the endowment and the spending to keep pace with inflation in the economy as a whole, in the absence of additional gifts to the endowment (see Chapter 3). To the extent that gifts contribute to growth, the spending rate might be raised. But in order to keep pace with the rate of inflation peculiar to higher education, the spending rate should probably be between 3 and 4 percent, although it might increase if gifts could be counted on for growth.

In setting a long-run spending rate based on long-run total-return expectations, it is important not to be overly influenced by short-run past performance. Table 5-1 shows five-year total return rates for the Standard & Poor's Composite Index (the "500" stock index) and suggests why, in the late 1960s, some boards of trustees mistakenly believed that high spending rates could be maintained and why, in the mid-1970s, some board may be too conservative.

Approval of a spending rate constitutes an important policy decision on the allocation of resources and, as such, is therefore a function of boards of trustees. But the board, as a practical matter, will probably be acting on the recommendation of the investment committee. The next step in developing a spending policy is the selection of a rule or formula by which the spending rate will be applied. This task may be performed by either a finance committee or an investment committee, but it depends heavily upon the judgments of both those committees.

ESTABLISHING A FORMULA

We have already seen the two objectives between which a spending formula should establish a reasonable compromise: stability in year-to-year spending and certainty of meeting the growth objectives of the endowment. There are limits to an institution's ability to adjust its budget up and down from year to year, and there are also limits to the willingness of trustees to risk a continuing decline in the value of the endowment fund. A third objective is the provision of some lead time for budgeting, so that the spending from endowment for a fiscal year can be determined well before the start of the fiscal year and time can be available for the preparation of budgets. It turns out that one

Table 5-1 Average Annual Total-Return Rates on Standard & Poor's Composite Index

PERIOD	AVERAGE ANNUAL TOTAL RETURN (%)
1950–54	23.7
1955–59	14.9
1960–64	10.5
1965–69	4.9
1970–74	−2.4

can satisfy this objective very easily without interfering with the other two.

Figure 5-1 illustrates the trade-offs between stability in spending and protection of growth in an endowment fund. All endowment funds have an element of risk, which is simply a consequence of the investment policy of the fund. If an institution is willing to put up with minimum spending stability, then the total risk in the endowment need be no greater than this investment risk. But as soon as the institution asks for more than minimum spending stability, some additional risk of failing to meet a growth target is introduced. And this risk increases as the institution demands greater stability in spending. As a practical matter, spending stability has a maximum, and it is therefore possible to estimate the total additional risk of achieving the ultimate in spending stability.

Minimum spending stability corresponds to a very simple spending rule that might be expressed in this way: Spend in each fiscal year 5 percent of what the market value of the endowment fund was on the first day of that year. Or, to provide for some budgeting lead, spend in each fiscal year 5 percent of what the market value of the endowment fund was six months prior to the beginning of that year.

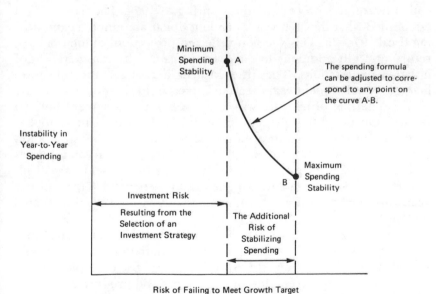

Source: Spending Policy for Educational Endowments, The Common Fund, 1975.

Figure 5-1. The Trade-Off between Stable Spending and Protecting Growth in an Endowment

If the value of the endowment fund drops by 20 percent from one year to the next, then spending from endowment also drops by 20 percent. For institutions heavily dependent upon spending from endowment, this kind of fluctuation is probably quite intolerable. The simplest way to reduce the fluctuations is to apply the spending rate not to a single market value of the endowment fund but to an average of several market values. So the spending rule might be modified to read this way: Spend in each fiscal year 5 percent of the average of three market values of the endowment fund—the value 6 months before the beginning of the fiscal year, the value 18 months before the beginning of the year, and the value 30 months before the beginning of the year.

A number of much more complex averaging formulas also have been proposed, and some are in use. But the research sponsored by The Common Fund suggests that none of these complicated methods offers any real advantage.

Maximum spending stability is achieved by abandoning the year-by-year use of the spending rate and the market value and simply budgeting a stable or perhaps steadily rising spending from endowment over future years. The starting point must be based on an appropriate spending rate and a market value. Dartmouth College embarked on this procedure in the spring of 1974. The trustees first established what they felt was a prudent dollar amount to spend during fiscal 1974–75. This decision reflected projections of total rates of return and gift additions to endowment as well as consideration of inflation expectations. Then the trustees authorized the college to budget for subsequent years regular increases in this dollar spending figure. The rate of increase was tentatively set at 6 percent but was revised downward to 4 percent in late 1974. Harvard University has followed much the same procedure, according to its Treasurer's Report for June 30, 1974. In late 1973, the Harvard deans and department heads were informed that the amounts they would have available for spending from endowment would increase at 4 percent per year until further notice. The budgets for 1974–75 were constructed on that basis.

Averaging several market values of the endowment funds provides stability in year-to-year spending. Lengthening the averaging period, increasing it from three to five years, for example, will increase the stability. Averaging over 10 years will produce something very close to maximum stability. Research for The Common Fund[19] suggested that averaging over five years will probably suit the needs of most institutions, but an institution can expect to gain no advantage by making use of monthly or quarterly rather than annual valuations.

The averaging process does require some adjustment of the spending rate. If it is appropriate to spend 5 percent of what the market value was at the beginning of a fiscal year, then it will be appropriate to spend a little more than 5 percent of the average of five market values because the market values will presumably rise over time. A detailed discussion of the adjustment is contained in The Common Fund report, and the adjustment formulas themselves appear in Appendix 9, as does a mathematical formulation of the averaging process discussed above.

Before settling on a spending formula, the finance committee or the investment committee will have to satisfy itself that the formula can be expected to achieve a reasonable balance between spending stability and likelihood of meeting the growth target for the endowment. (The simulation approach described in The Common Fund report is the best way to test the probable consequences of any particular spending formula.) Perhaps, given the investment policy chosen for the endowment fund (and the expectation of gift additions to the fund), no spending formula can achieve a balance that seems appropriate to the finance and investment committees. In this case, it may be necessary to modify the investment policy or perhaps the development effort. It is critical that there be consistency among the investment policy, the spending formula, and the spending conditions that are acceptable to the institution.

VI/*Endowment Fund Accounting and Reporting*

The past two or three years have seen expressions of growing discontent over the manner in which educational institutions report on their financial operations. Some of this criticism has appeared in print; probably more of it has appeared in the complaints of alumni frustrated in their efforts to comprehend what is going on at their own institutions. By and large, this issue has been overshadowed by the controversy over investment practices and spending policies for endowment funds. But in the spring of 1973, an academic critique of college and university reporting practices, picked up and exploited by both *The Wall Street Journal* and *Newsweek* magazine, created a furor that, although brief, was painful to a number of institutions.

Much of the expressed dissatisfaction involved the matter of accounting for costs, a subject somewhat removed from endowment funds. But much controversy has concerned aspects of accounting and reporting that are very much involved with endowment funds. And it is through institutional reporting that the constituencies of an institution, particularly its alumni and potential donors, form their impressions of the way in which endowment funds are being managed. Indeed, an institution may well discover that its reporting practices regarding the management of its endowment fund are just as important to relations with alumni and donors as the investment and spending policies themselves.[1] Probably the two most important questions the reader of a report may ask on this subject are how profitably has the endowment fund been managed; and, in view of the performance record and the needs of the institution, how prudent is the spending from the endowment that has taken place?

The reader may also wish to know what portion of the total budget of the institution is being carried by the endowment fund. He may be interested in whether this portion is changing over time, *131* whether the endowment fund is continuing to carry its share of the total budget as costs rise over the years. He may want to know to what extent gifts are increasing the endowment, and he may want some idea of the overall investment policy or the strategy of the endowment. These questions can serve as criteria for college and university financial reporting practices and as a basis for evaluating the recent criticism and the suggestions for change.

PROPOSALS FOR CHANGE

In recent years, three publications have appeared that deal with college and university accounting and reporting: the Report of the American Accounting Association Committee, published in 1971;[2] a working paper by Professors Harold Bierman, Jr., and Thomas R. Hofstedt on university accounting and deficits;[3] and the *Industry Audit Guide: Audits of Colleges and Universities*, developed by the Committee on College and University Accounting and Auditing of the American Institute of Certified Public Accountants, with the help of the National Association of College and University Business Officers, published in 1973.[4]

Although the Report of the Committee on Accounting Practice has nothing to say about accounting for endowment funds specifically, its general criticism of college and university accounting practices has a bearing on reporting for endowment funds. The summary of recommendations begins with this statement:

> The recommendations of this Committee are based on its conclusions that current accounting and reporting practices of most NFP [not-for-profit] organizations, being almost exclusively evolved from and focused upon legalistic dollar accountability for individual funds entities on a year-by-year basis, often lack relevance and freedom from bias and do not adequately fulfill the objectives of accounting.

The report goes on to state that this fund-by-fund accounting neglects the operating entity as a whole.

The Bierman and Hofstedt paper is the one that was publicized by *The Wall Street Journal* in April 1973, and by *Newsweek* in May 1973. Bierman and Hofstedt were critical of a number of features of college and university accounting and reporting, and much of the criticism was perfectly justified, although the practices they criticized have largely disappeared since the adoption of the *Audit Guide*. But one of their recommendations was taken up and misinterpreted by the two magazines.

It would be convenient if one could identify for a college or university a single measure of financial health, and one is tempted to look in a financial report for the single number that is most revealing. Until the adoption of the *Audit Guide,* many institutions reported a "surplus" or "deficit," and many readers of financial statements fixed upon this number as the key to an institution's financial health. In their criticism of the reporting of deficits by Ivy League universities, Bierman and Hofstedt alleged that, in many cases, "their financial reports continue to reflect accounting conventions that obscure rather than illuminate the magnitude of financial problems."[5] They recommended that a university report something closely analogous to the "income" of a business corporation, and they defined "income" as the "money value of the net accretion to one's economic power between two points in time." Specifically, they proposed an income statement for a university that would begin by reporting "operating income" as revenues from educational and related activities, less expenses and interest on debt but before receipts from endowment and before gifts. Then the university's total income would be computed by adding to operating income the sum of gifts, the income yield on endowment, and the appreciation on endowment less expenses of administering the endowment.

Newsweek and *The Wall Street Journal* picked up this concept of total income, because the figures presented by Bierman and Hofstedt indicated that total income (including all appreciation on endowment funds) for the Ivy League institutions had been very substantial in 1970–71, when many of these institutions had been reporting deficits. The implication in the magazine articles was that the institutions were indeed making a great deal of money, although they complained that they could not break even. Some readers drew the further inference that an institution should increase its spending in years of substantial endowment appreciation and reduce it in years of substantial depreciation in order to produce a reasonable and consistent total income figure.

Bierman and Hofstedt did not intend to suggest any such thing. But it was natural to draw this inference from their recommendation, given people's natural desire for a single true measure of financial strength.[6]

The *Industry Audit Guide: Audits of Colleges and Universities* was prepared by the Committee of the American Institute of Certified Public Accountants on College and University Accounting and Auditing and was published in 1973. The preface to the *Audit Guide* says:

This guide has been prepared to assist the independent auditor in examining and reporting on financial statements of nonprofit institutions of higher education including colleges, universities and community or junior colleges.[7]

And in its Notice to Readers, the *Audit Guide* says:

> This Audit Guide is published for the guidance of members of the Institute in examining and reporting on the financial statements of colleges and universities. It represents the considered opinion of the Committee on College and University Accounting and Auditing and as such contains the best thought of the profession as to the best practices in this area of financial reporting. Members should be aware that they may be called upon to justify departures from the Committee's recommendations.[8]

The *Audit Guide* appears to have had a substantial impact on the preparation of college and university financial statements. The June 30, 1974, financial reports of many colleges and universities specifically mention the *Audit Guide* and state that the institutions have changed their reporting practices to conform to its recommendations. And a number of these recommendations have to do with endowment funds.

The *Audit Guide* deals with three basic financial statements for colleges and universities: the balance sheet, the statement of changes in funds balance, and the statement of current funds revenues, expenditures, and other changes (which I shall refer to as the statement of current funds revenues). Endowment funds figure in all three of these. The balance sheet shows the assets of endowment and similar funds, and shows as fund balances the balances for three components: true endowment, term endowment, and quasi endowment. The statement of changes in fund balances shows increases in endowment due to realized gains, transfers from other funds, and gifts, and decreases due to transfers to current funds. The current funds revenues statement shows as revenue the income yield on endowment and similar funds and as a transfer to current funds any further spending from endowment. It also shows as a transfer from current funds to quasi endowment any reinvestment of income yield.

Chapter 8 of the *Audit Guide* deals with "Endowment and Similar Funds," broken down into endowment funds, term-endowment funds, and quasi-endowment funds. These terms mean respectively true-endowment funds, true-endowment funds that will at some point in time become expendable as to principal, and funds on which principal may legally be spent. The *Audit Guide* indicates that totals for each of these three categories should be shown on the fund balance side of the balance sheet, ordinarily at book value (that is, at cost adjusted for realized gains and losses):

> Investments purchased usually are reported in the financial statements at cost and investments received as gifts at the fair market or appraised value at the date of gift. . . . [But] as a permissible alternative, investments, exclusive of physical plant, may be reported in the financial statements at current market value or fair value, provided this basis is used for all investments of all funds.[9]

The investment performance of endowment funds is singled out for reporting. The *Audit Guide* says that "the financial statements or notes should set forth the total performance (i.e., yield and gains and losses) of the investment portfolio based on cost and market value."[10] (Market value alone is apparently acceptable.) It is not entirely clear whether the reference to gains and losses includes unrealized as well as realized gains and losses. The reference to cost and market value suggests that both realized and unrealized gains and losses should be reported. From these figures, the reader of a financial statement could at least make an estimate of the percent yield and percent total return achieved for the year. But better information may be available. If endowment funds are pooled, the *Audit Guide* states that the basis of income distribution requires that the pool be unitized on a market-value basis. And in its sample note to financial statements, the *Audit Guide* suggests reporting for a *pooled* endowment fund both total market value and cost at the beginning and end of the year, both realized and unrealized net gain for the year, market value per unit at the beginning and end of the year, and earned income per unit.[11]

The statement of current funds revenues is, according to the *Audit Guide*,

> unique to educational and similar institutions. It is a statement of financial activities of current funds related to the current reporting period showing the details of current funds revenues by source, current funds expenditures by function, and all other changes in current funds.[12]

This statement will probably be seen by most readers as roughly analogous to the income statement of a business, but the *Audit Guide* warns, "It does not purport to present the results of operations or the net income or loss for the period as would a statement of income or a statement of revenues and expenses."[13] Essentially, the statement enables a reader to see what the institution spent money on and where that money came from. It should enable the reader to see the relative importance of different sources of revenues, including tuition, current gifts, and spending from endowment.

The statement breaks revenues down into three columns: unrestricted, restricted, and total. One item of revenue is endowment income, broken down, of course, into unrestricted and restricted components. The *Audit Guide* defines "endowment income" as excluding gains and losses on the endowment fund. An institution that spends a portion of gains in addition to income yield reports that portion as a transfer and does not include it in endowment income. This stipulation reflects the traditional accounting view that the endowment income includes only conventional income yield. The *Audit Guide* definition of endowment income does not conflict with the Uniform Management of Institutional Funds Act, which permits the spending of a prudent portion of gains on endowment funds but does not define endowment income. But it may conflict with some state statutes that define "income" to include a portion of gains or leave it to the governing body of an institution to determine what income is, although auditors are apparently willing to accept the statutory definition without giving an "exception."

The *Audit Guide* defines "endowment income" as *income earned* and not necessarily *income distributed*. Some institutions make a practice of establishing an income reserve, frequently designating an endowment income stabilization reserve, to which income yield is diverted in some years and from which income is spent in other years. But the *Audit Guide* makes it clear that what is reported as endowment income is not what happens to be spent during a fiscal year but what the earned income is on the endowment fund.

Any spending of gains on endowment funds is in the statement of current funds revenues as a *transfer*, and the example given by the *Audit Guide* is "portion of unrestricted quasi-endowment gains appropriated." This categorization appears to overlook one important aspect of appropriation of endowment funds to meet current expenditures and takes us back to the deficit problem.

If an institution has decided to expend a prudent portion of gains from an endowment fund (the Uniform Management of Institutional Funds Act speaks in terms of cumulative gains, not just gains of a particular fiscal year), it reports the transfer of that prudent portion and *probably* (although not necessarily) reports a deficit only if that transfer is not sufficient to close the gap between total revenues and transfers and total expenditures. But in this latter case, the only way to deal with the deficit (if it is a cash deficit) may be through a *further* transfer from endowment, a transfer beyond what has originally been planned as prudent. Probably this transfer will be from quasi-endowment funds. The *Audit Guide* does not clearly indicate whether an institution should report two separate transfers in this case and label them to distinguish their purposes. Some trustees may be troubled by the prospect of wrestling first with the problem of determining a prudent amount to spend from endowment and then with how to explain spending beyond a level of prudence.

Should the institution spend *less* than its earned income, the *Audit Guide* appears to regard the appropriate entry as a transfer from unrestricted current funds to quasi-endowment funds. At this point, a number of institutions have traditionally added a portion of earned income to an income stabilization reserve. As the *Audit Guide* says:

> Some institutions have created such reserves by setting aside a portion of the income earned by pooled investments. In any given year, the distribution to the income accounts of participating funds from pooled earnings was made at a fixed or predetermined rate more or less than the actual earnings for the period. The difference was added to or deducted from the reserve for stabilization of income.[14]

The *Audit Guide* is opposed to this practice, although the use of the reserve is not necessarily objectionable. It is certainly difficult to tell whether a college or university *has* spent less than the income from endowment and similar funds, because many kinds of unrestricted revenues go into unrestricted current funds and many expenses and transfers come out. Some institutions apparently have followed a practice of not reporting all income earned during the year and disclosing only the income spent. And some have failed to identify the restricted and unrestricted portions of the stabilization reserve. Both failures were the source of the *Audit Guide* proscription of stabilization reserves. But an institution may still use a stabilization reserve and make the desired allocations and disclosures. The 1974 edition of *College and University Business Administration* follows the principles of the *Audit Guide* but says it is acceptable to report all endowment income earned as revenue and then to show a transfer to the unrestricted current funds balance—allocated, corresponding to the income added to the reserve.[15] The reserve itself would be reported as an allocated portion of the unrestricted current funds balance on the institution's balance sheet. (Unspent restricted income would automatically show up in the current restricted funds balance.) In short, the requirement, if trustees decided to set aside a portion of the unrestricted income from endowment and similar funds, would have to either be transferred to quasi endowment from unrestricted current funds balance or remain as an identified item in that balance.

College and university financial reports for fiscal 1973–74 display a variety of practices. Some institutions have terminated their reserves by simply transferring the balance to the unrestricted current funds balance. Others have hidden them or at least disguised them (probably not intentionally but in an effort to follow the *Audit Guide*) by incorporating them anonymously in the unrestricted current funds balance. The reader cannot tell in such a case whether the institution has deliberately held back some endowment income from spending. And some institutions have preserved clearly labeled stabilization reserves as a part of the restricted or unrestricted funds balance. Some use the term "undistributed endowment income" as the label.

The statement of changes in fund balances shows increases due to realized gains on investments and transfers from other funds, such as annuity and life income funds, as well as transfers of investment income from unrestricted current funds to endowment. Gift and bequest additions to endowment are handled in two ways. A gift that the donor designates for endowment, whether or not the income from the gift is restricted to a particular purpose, appears as an addition to endowment in the statement of changes in fund balances, under gifts and bequests—restricted. A gift that is not designated for endowment and for which income is not restricted but which the trustees decide to add to quasi endowment is shown as revenue in unrestricted current funds and as a transfer from unrestricted current funds to endowment, under unrestricted gifts allocated.

The statement of changes in fund balances also shows deductions *from* endowment funds. Two examples given in the *Audit Guide* are the transfer of a portion of gains appropriated for expenditure (which shows up in the statement of current funds revenues not as revenue but as a *transfer* to unrestricted current funds) and expired term endowments, removed from endowment funds and shown as a separately identified *revenue* item in the statement of current funds revenues.

The *Audit Guide*, in the course of lengthy discussion of the total-return concept, expresses a good deal of concern about the practice of appropriating a portion of capital gains for current expenditure:

> The law and the legal profession, while by no means in accord on the subject, appear to be heading in the direction of elimination of limitations on the governing board's right to appropriate gains for expenditure. The total return concept continues, however, to cause accountants difficulty in that the concept thus far has pro-

duced few, if any, practical applications which appear to be *objectively determinable*. No clear *redefinition* of traditional income yield has evolved. The exercise of prudence is subjective and not susceptible to measurement in an accounting sense. The practical applications of the total return concept utilized to date amount substantively to the selection of a "spending rate" usually relating the rate to the market value of the portfolio. They appear in some cases to involve an intolerable element of arbitrariness. Consequently, until a general practice evolves which is *objectively determinable*, the Guide would do a disservice to higher education and the accounting profession to sanction as a permissible accounting treatment the inclusion in revenue of gains utilized under a total return approach. Therefore, any portion of gains utilized should be reported in the financial statement as a transfer. . . . The fact that this Guide does not sanction recognition of appropriated gains as revenues should not inhibit the application of the total return policy of investment management, a policy which has economic merit.[16]

The last sentence of the quotation expresses support for total return as an investment strategy but takes no position with respect to a spending policy that makes use of yield and gain. The *Audit Guide* was concerned with the definition of "income," not with the establishment of prudent-spending rules.

CURRENT ACCOUNTING AND REPORTING OF COLLEGES AND UNIVERSITIES

An examination of a sampling of college and university financial reports for the fiscal year ending June 30, 1974, reveals a wide variation in methods of accounting and reporting and in the usefulness of what is presented.

An obvious question to which a reader of a financial report should find answers concerns the investment performance of the endowment fund. How profitably has it been run? The best answer to this question will come either in the form of a percentage rate of return, perhaps broken into yield and appreciation components, or unit values and unit incomes. The unitization of an endowment fund (see Chapter III) consists of treating an endowment fund as a mutual fund is treated, with the calculation and reporting of the value per unit or per share and the income per unit. From these figures one can compute yield, appreciation, and total return.

A few institutions report both the unit value and the income per unit, either for their entire endowment fund or for components of their endowments. California Institute of Technology, Harvard University, Radcliffe College, Stanford University, Swarthmore College, The University of California, Smith College, and The University of Rochester are among the institutions providing this complete information. Some of these reports show the unit values and unit incomes as of June 30, 1973, and June 30, 1974. Others give a history of unit values and unit incomes over several years.

Still other institutions, including Yale and Amherst, furnish unit values for their endowment funds but not unit income figures. So, one can deduce the rate of appreciation in the fund year-by-year for several years, but the income yield and hence the rate of total return are difficult to determine. The Yale Treasurer's Report presents the total return as a percent, giving the reader the means of determining the income yield, the rate of appreciation, and the total-return rate. Amherst supplies a projected yield percent as of June 30, 1974.

The next level of reporting provides market values for the total endowment fund at the beginning of the year and at the end of the year, together with a statement of transfers into and out of the fund. This information can provide the basis for a fairly good estimate of the rate of investment appreciation on the fund. The reader must adjust the change in market value to include the effect of transfers and make some assumptions about when those transfers might have taken place during the year, assumptions that are not very critical if the transfers were small in relation to the total size of the endowment. If the presentation of the transfers is a good one, as it generally is for the institutions that have adopted the recommendations of the *Audit Guide,* then it is not very difficult to deduce an approximate rate of appreciation or depreciation on the endowment fund. But this deduction does involve some expertise and a number of calculations. If the financial report also states the amount of income received on the endowment fund, it is possible to estimate the yield percentage, although this calculation becomes somewhat tricky if transfers in and out of the endowment fund have been substantial. The sum of the rate of appreciation and the rate of yield is the total-return rate. It is not always easy to determine the exact amount of income on the endowment fund. Some institutions report "income from investments," but investments are not necessarily the same as endowment funds. Other institutions report "income availed of," which refers to the amount of money earned on the endowment (not necessarily in the fiscal year) and actually spent, which may be more or less than the income actually earned. Income availed of will not help in determining the investment performance of an endowment fund.

The next level of reporting describes the endowment fund only in terms of book value (i.e., cost adjusted by realized gains and losses), rather than market value. Book values provide no indication of the investment performance of the endowment. Even if market values at year end are indicated in a footnote, without the transfer information one cannot arrive at even an approximation of investment performance.

For institutions that do not follow the traditional spending rule, which calls for spending precisely the income yield on an endowment fund, one also would like to know how much the trustees have decided to spend. This information enables one to judge whether the institution is jeopardizing its future through excessive current spending or perhaps jeopardizing its present quality by unduly favoring future spending.

A few institutions, Swarthmore and Smith among them, have furnished a very detailed discussion of their philosophy with respect to investment policy and spending policy for endowment funds. The Yale Treasurer's Reports for 1965–66 and for 1966–67 set out the new Yale philosophy. Subsequent treasurers' reports have offered further commentary, but in order to understand fully the Yale position, one must go back to one of these earlier reports.

The Harvard Treasurer's Report for June 30, 1974, includes a detailed discussion of Harvard's thinking with respect to spending policy for endowment funds, but again, a reader of a Harvard report five years hence may have to refer to the 1974 report to understand what Harvard is about. Smith, on the other hand, continues to describe its philosophy in detail five years after it was adopted, furnishing an up-to-date evaluation of its getting and spending.

Harvard and Stanford report investment performance in the form of unit value and income per unit, and also distribution, the amount actually drawn down and spent, per unit. Some other institutions, including Yale, show the number of dollars received as income yield and spent and the number of dollars spent in excess of this income yield. Provided that one is able to compute a total-return rate and to determine the total spending as a rate, one can make judgments concerning spending policy. The Yale Treasurer's Report provides the data necessary for these calculations, but many other institutions' reports do not.

For some other universities, the extent of spending above or below income yield is revealed only in the form of transfers to and from the endowment fund, which are not always labeled so that one can tell that these were in effect the reinvestment of income yield or spending in excess of income yield. In these cases, only by luck will a reader be able to determine true spending from endowment, and even then he may not have data on investment performance against which to judge this spending.

The reader of a financial report has good reason to want to know how much of the institution's budget is being carried by the endowment fund and whether this fraction is rising or falling over time. A large number of the financial reports examined give a reasonable answer to the first question, but relatively few are helpful with respect to the second.

The reports that give the most trouble are those that do not clearly distinguish between income yield earned on the endowment fund and spending from the endowment fund. The latter is the measure of the institution's dependence on the endowment fund to meet budget needs for the fiscal year. But it is sometimes difficult to tell from the financial report just what this latter amount was. Yale's report is probably the clearest on this point, showing separately the income yield that was used by the university and the portion of appreciation that was used.

CONCLUSION

The *Audit Guide* has brought about an enormous improvement in the formal reporting of colleges and universities and in the standardizing of these reports to permit reasonable comparability among institutions. In avoiding any identification of surplus or deficit, the *Audit Guide* has helped to make the point that there simply is no single measure of financial performance.

One important matter that the *Audit Guide* does not deal with, because it is not strictly an accounting issue, concerns the level of spending from endowment and whether it is appropriate to the needs and limitations of the institution. If reporting of income yield follows the *Audit Guide*, it will generally be complete and accurate. But not all institutions spend precisely this income yield, and, for those that do, it is not necessarily a prudent amount to spend.

Finally, although the *Audit Guide* sets out formal requirements, the college and university financial report must generally serve a variety of purposes beyond formal presentation of accounts. It can help to explain financial needs to faculty and students and enlist their aid in maintaining and strengthening the institution, and it can communicate to the donors and potential donors who are critical to the survival of most private higher education both the need for support and the competence with which resources are managed.

Appendixes

1. DEFERRED GIVING: GIFT ANNUITIES AND LIFE INCOME FUNDS[1]

College and university endowment funds can benefit significantly from gift annuities and life income (so-called charitable remainder) gifts. Largely a result of the Tax Reform Act of 1969, the tax rules governing these very specialized forms of gift are extremely complex. To make use of these gifts, a college or university will need considerable expertise within its administrative staff and will have to decide from time to time which programs are appropriate.[2] This appendix is no substitute for that expertise.

The trustees of some institutions may be apprehensive that emphasizing deferred giving will lead to a reduction in gifts of immediate benefit to the institution. But at least some colleges have found that donors of deferred gifts not only maintain their regular gifts but also become more interested in making additional deferred gifts, including bequests. And unlike promised bequests, annuity and life income gifts offer certainty of receipt and an opportunity for the institution to invest the gift for growth over the donor's lifetime.

The Charitable Gift Annuity

This device combines a tax-deductible gift with the purchase of a life annuity. The donor/purchaser makes a single payment, part of which represents a gift and part of which represents the cost of an annuity, to the institution, which in return provides him with a fixed annuity (which may be paid monthly, quarterly, semiannually, or annually but is usually quarterly or semiannual) for life.

In offering these annuities, colleges and universities are not really competing with life insurance companies, because part of the payment to the educational institution is a gift. If the same total payment were made to a life insurance company, the amount would purchase a larger annuity.

145

Most educational institutions base the payment for their annuities on uniform tables prepared by the committee on gift annuities.[3] These tables set the payment so that it will cover the cost of the annuity over the lives of the people involved and will leave the institution a sum equal to about half the original payment, to be added to endowment.

An institution should give some thought to the expenses of operating a gift annuity program, especially if state laws require extensive record keeping and segregation of reserves for the protection of the annuitants. But a gift annuity program may be cheaper to operate than a program of life income trusts.

The gift element covers the possibility that the annuitants may outlive the life expectancy reflected in the tables and probably provides enough protection against a loss so that the institution does not need the expertise of a life insurance company to set up a gift annuity program. But some states regulate the sale of annuities by colleges and universities.

For tax purposes, the gift to the institution is the difference between the payment made by the donor/purchaser and the "cost" of the annuity, which is determined from U.S. Treasury tables and is approximately what a commercial insurance company would charge for annuity.[4] The annuitant pays income tax on a portion of the annuity, just as if he had purchased it from a life insurance company for a premium equal to the cost according to the Treasury tables.[5]

The payment to the institution can take the form of cash, appreciated securities or real estate, or other property. But like outright gifts, charitable gift annuity payments in forms other than cash or securities pose some complicated tax problems. And if the donor/purchaser uses appreciated property to cover both the gift element and the cost portion of the payment, then he may incur a capital gains tax.[6]

The annuity may be payable over the life of someone other than the donor/purchaser or over his life and then over the life of someone else. In such cases, the donor/purchaser may have to pay gift tax on the "cost" of the annuity that is payable to other persons. And annuity receipts that pass to another person on the death of the donor/purchaser are subject to an estate tax.[7]

The donor/purchaser need not purchase the gift annuity during his own lifetime; he may create it in favor of a beneficiary under his will. In this case, the charitable gift portion of the bequest establishing the annuity is deductible for estate tax purposes.[8]

Or the donor/purchaser may set up a "deferred payment gift annuity," delaying the start of the annuity for a year or more after he makes his payment. The donor/purchaser may then take the charitable gift deduction in a year during which he is in a high tax bracket and receive the annuity later, in years of lower tax rates.[9] (The committee on gift annuities has a set of recommended calculations for adjusting the annuity and the payment to allow for the deferral.)

The Life Income Gift

Under this arrangement, the donor makes a gift to the institution but continues to receive the income on the gift for himself for life or for a fixed period of up to 20 years. Or, as in the case of the annuity, the income may be paid out over the lives of more than one person. When the payments of income come to an end, the remaining balance of the gift can be added to the institution's endowment; hence the terms "charitable remainder gift" and, in the Internal Revenue Code, "charitable remainder trusts."[10]

The donor obtains a tax deduction for the portion of his gift that represents the charitable remainder. The income recipient generally pays income tax on what he receives. Except in the special case of tax-exempt unitrusts, the donor escapes any long-term capital gains tax on a gift of appreciated securities, and the gift may function as a tax-free conversion of low-yield appreciated securities into a high-yield trust.

There are three general classes of life income trusts: the annuity trust, the unitrust, and the pooled life income fund. Annuity trusts are similar to charitable gift annuities. But the charitable gift annuity—for which the gift component becomes part of the institution's endowment—rather than a separate trust or fund is an unconditional obligation of the institution. Whereas the life income annuity trust is separately invested, and if its assets are exhausted through a combination of poor investment results and annuity payments, then the annuity ceases.

The Life Income Unitrust

The "unitrust" is a separately invested trust with a separate portfolio of securities and a trust document describing in detail the income payment arrangements. Under the Internal Revenue Code and Regulations, these arrangements may take one of three forms.

The first method fixes the annual income at a specified portion (not less than 5 percent) of the market value of the trust assets as revalued each year. Payments must be made at least annually and are usually made quarterly or semiannually. Market value usually fluctuates, and the dollar amount of income varies accordingly. When the required distribution exceeds the income earned by the trust assets, some of the principal of the trust must be distributed to the beneficiary. As far as the beneficiary's own taxes are concerned, these distributions from principal are treated either as capital gains distributions[11] or as a tax-free return of principal. The unitrust is itself exempt from income tax, so that if it can make the income payments to the beneficiary and still grow in value, this growth will be free of tax.

The second, so-called net-income method limits the income received by the beneficiary to the actual income earned by the trust assets, up to a stated percentage (at least 5 percent) of the market value determined each year.

The third method is referred to as "net-income-plus-makeup." This method is similar to the net-income method, but in any year in which the trust income exceeds the stated percentage, the excess is paid out to the beneficiary to the extent that aggregate payments in earlier years have been less than the stated percentage. In other words, low income payments in early years can be made up in later years if the income of the trust rises.

The fixed-income method, unlike the net-income and net-income-plus-makeup methods, poses the risk that if the specified percentage is set too high, the result may be a depletion of the capital of the gift. Some caution is clearly called for in quoting percentage payout rates.

The trustee (which is usually the college or university but may be another institution, a bank, or an individual) makes investment decisions for the unitrust and can change the investment objectives over time. Nothing prevents investment of trust assets or a portion of them in tax-exempt municipal bonds, the interest on which would be tax-exempt to the beneficiary. (The net-income distribution method would be the best here because the distribution would always match the tax-exempt interest.) But the transfer of appreciated securities to a unitrust, so that they could be sold for reinvestment in tax-exempt securities, would result in taxable capital gains to the donor.[12]

The unitrust can be set up to make income payments over the lives of the income beneficiaries or for a fixed period of up to 20 years. And the donor can make additional contributions to the unitrust after the initial gift.

When a donor sets up a unitrust, he obtains a charitable deduction for the fair market value of the remainder interest, the amount that can be expected ultimately to pass to the college or university. The calculation of this deduction is based upon Treasury regulations and tables, which make use of the life expectancies of the income beneficiaries, the income payout percentage, and the assumption that the trust assets will earn 6 percent a year. Unitrusts are usually set up with gifts of long-term appreciated securities, and the donor escapes capital gains tax (unless the unitrust is to be invested in tax-exempt securities).

The expenses of managing unitrusts should be carefully considered. Most institutions do not like to charge the income beneficiary more than a modest amount for management (and some do not charge at all), but the right to charge reasonable expenses is usually reserved in the trust instrument. Separately managed trusts require a good deal of record keeping and investment management on an individual basis. Until an institution has enough unitrusts to justify having its own "trust officer," it may be wise to put all the management and record keeping in the hands of a bank. Some banks make a special effort to handle just this kind of business.

Pooled Life Income Funds

A number of separate life income trusts may be pooled for investment management purposes. Each trust then owns a portion of a single portfolio and is entitled to its pro rata share of the income of the pooled portfolio. (The pool must be unitized on a market-value basis.) An institution may maintain more than one life income pool, and differing investment objectives can offer the donor a choice. For example, Harvard offers the John Harvard Fund for maximum current income and the Veritas Fund for appreciation and less immediate income. Dartmouth College has a high-yield pool offering substantial income with little prospect of growth and a balanced pool offering a more modest income with some growth prospect. Treasury regulations prohibit investing a pooled fund in tax-exempt securities.

Some institutions pool life income trusts with general endowment funds. Regulations based on the Tax Reform Act of 1969 permit such pooling only if the principal and income interests of the life income trusts can be clearly distinguished from those interests of the institutional funds.[13] In starting up a pooled life income fund, an institution may invest some of its own funds as seed money. But a long-term commingling of life income funds and regular endowment can lead to difficulties, because the appropriate investment objectives for the two kinds of funds are generally not the same. For the same reason, some trustees feel strongly that the trustee of a pooled life income fund should *not* be the institution itself.

Distributions from a pooled fund are always taxable to the respective beneficiaries as ordinary income.

The pooled life income fund is "owned" by the separate life income trusts, each of which was set up by a donor. As in the case of the unitrust, the donor may specify that the income for his trust is to be payable to him or to some other person for life and then to a number of survivors for life. (He does not have the option of receiving income payments over a term of years, as he would with a unitrust.) When the last of these survivors has died, the particular trust comes to an end, and its share of the assets in the pooled fund is transferred to the regular endowment fund of the institution.

This transfer is the charitable remainder. When the donor makes the gift that establishes the life income trust, the fair market value of this remainder constitutes a tax deduction as a charitable gift. As in the case of the unitrust, this value is determined from Treasury tables based on the ages of the beneficiaries. But although the calculation for the unitrust is based on the income payment percentage specified in the trust agreement, the deduction for a gift that enters a pooled fund is based on the actual payout experience of the particular pool. For a new pooled fund (less than three taxable years old), the deductible portion of gifts to the pool is based on an arbitrary payout of 6 percent. After three years, the computation must be based on the highest annual yield of the preceding three years. If the yield from a new pool is likely to exceed 6 percent, the donor will obtain a larger deduction if he makes his gift during the first three years of the pool when the deduction is computed at 6 percent.

Pooled life income funds offer some investment management efficiencies that are not possible for the separately invested unitrusts, and it is probably better for the institution if a gift can be pooled. At one time, there was a question about whether offering a pooled fund participation might constitute the "sale" of a security and hence require registration under federal securities laws. But the Securities and Exchange Commission has issued a "no action" letter, conditioning freedom from SEC regulation on complete disclosure of the investment objectives and practices of the particular pooled fund to all donors, prospective donors, and beneficiaries.

Remainder in a Residence or Farm

This type of gift is somewhat esoteric but may suit the preferences of a donor who wishes a college or university to have his home or farm on his death (or the death of another person) and prefers to complete the gift before that death. The donor may transfer title to the institution and retain for himself, and another if he wishes, the right to live in the house or work the farm for life or a term of years. He obtains a charitable deduction for the value of the property less straight line depreciation over the relevant life expectancy or term of years, discounted at 6 percent over the life expectancy or terms of years.[14]

The donor and the institution will have to negotiate payments of property taxes, insurance, and other costs of maintenance of the property. Usually, the tenant continues to bear such costs.

2. EXAMPLES OF INVESTMENT OBJECTIVES

Two sets of objectives are given here, as examples of what some institutions are doing rather than as models to be followed. The first comes from a small private college with an endowment in the $25 million to $50 million range and is accompanied by explanatory comments from the investment committee of the trustees. (Some minor alterations have been made to avoid identifying the college.) This college has delegated the day-to-day management of its endowment to an outside investment counseling firm, and the statement of objectives serves as a set of instructions to the manager.

The second set of objectives comes from Harvard University, which has the largest endowment in the country. Almost all of the endowment is managed by the Harvard Management Company, which is wholly owned by Harvard, but some funds have been turned over to outside professionals for day-to-day management. The statement of objectives deals with the overall policy for both inside- and outside-managed funds.

Example 1. Investment Objectives of a Private College

The objectives of investment management are to produce on average over the next decade (or longer) a total return of 11 percent per annum of which at least 4 percent should be in the form of yield (interest and dividends) and 7 percent in the form of appreciation. The spending rate has been set at 5 percent of a thirteen-quarter moving average of market value. The standard deviation of the total return should not exceed 9 percent. No withdrawals need be anticipated for at least the next decade.

The objective is, of course, to have spending increase at an average rate of at least 6 percent per annum to offset the assumed inflation rate of educational institutions. An income equalization reserve account will be maintained to smooth the rate of increase in spending.

All assets will be carried at market values and marked to market to calculate returns for each quarterly period. No distinction will be made between realized and unrealized gains and losses. For budgeting purposes, three years of results are relevant; for the measurement of performance, a full market cycle will be the period.

The objectives have been set at a level which, we have agreed, does not require exposure to risks of permanent capital losses. Quality standards will be maintained so that bonds and stock selections are always being made from the upper two-thirds of the quality range. Periodic reports will at least twice a year show how this quality standard is being determined and met.

Without special authorization, no equity security shall represent more than 10 percent of the stock portfolio and the ten largest holdings will not represent more than 50 percent of the total.

The asset mix of the portfolio will range within the following limits:

Cash equivalents	0 to 30%
Bonds or mortgages	15% to 30%
Common stocks and securities convertible into equity	55% to 85%

Any of these limits can be changed on a showing that an adjustment is needed.

Comments from the Investment Committee

Certain measures can be further refined. For example, the portfolio beta and the R^2 can be established for the common stock portfolio and for the entire portfolio to measure both possible variability and diversification. The alphas should probably not be estimated in advance but left to measure the quality of specific security selection by the investment manager.*

Individual agency ratings for bonds and stocks can be used to suggest some classification of quality but a more precise ranking is necessary to assure control over this critical variable. In the case of subordinated convertible debt instruments, of course, the rating system is not applicable to an arbitraging activity.

---

*Editor's Note: The "beta" is the volatility discussed in Chapter 2; the R^2 measures the closeness of fit of the stock portfolio performance and the stock market performance. The "alpha" is the intercept of a line of best fit.

In the preceding definition of objectives, a decision was made to hold asset quality high and to permit a large position in common stocks. This was based upon forecasts of equity returns and their expected distribution among quality grades. The alternative might have been a smaller proportion of more risky and variable stocks to achieve the same general portfolio profile. This kind of refinement in the distribution of assets could be captured only by a more precise asset distribution than the conventional cash equivalent, bond, and common stock breakdown.

Similarly, the maturity structure of the bond portfolio is not specified as an objective: Rather these details of portfolio structure are matters of managerial discretion in response to changing market relationships and expected near-term developments. For this reason, a range of objectives is to be preferred to an overly precise statement which restricts the range of alternative combinations of assets of different types.

The statement of objectives also serves to indicate the reliance to be placed on timing: very little. Our presumption is that the manager has no special talent for timing and that it will not be relied upon to contribute to the level and stability of total return. At the margin, however, room is left for making modest shifts in the portfolio position on the basis of interest rate and stock market forecasts. The limits on such shifts are a specific statement of unwillingness to rely upon a timing as opposed to a long-term investing strategy.

Example 2. Harvard University Investment Objectives

INVESTMENT OBJECTIVES
HARVARD ENDOWMENT

Introduction

From its founding in 1636, Harvard has been an endowed institution. Initially its assets were John Harvard's books and a few British pounds. Over the last three centuries countless generous individuals wishing to support private higher education have contributed to Harvard's endowment. Through a combination of personal generosity, prudent spending and successful investment management Harvard's General Investments Account (the "Fund") has grown to well over one billion dollars, making it the largest of its kind in the world. Over time many forms of investment media have been in the Fund, but in recent decades it has consisted primarily of investments in common stocks and bonds of major U.S. corporations.

The Fund is made up of various restricted and unrestricted funds which own units in the Fund operated as a single commingled pool. The income generated by the Fund serves to support educational purposes in the undergraduate college and the various graduate schools and related institutions. Annually the endowment income supports between 20–25% of the University's operating budget, which is currently approaching $250 million. The management of the Fund is governed by Massachusetts law, including its "Prudent Man" Rule. Only income in the form of interest and dividends is currently spent. Realized and unrealized capital gains are treated as additions to principal.

Gifts continue to play a critical role both for current spending and growth. On an annual basis historically there has been an inflow of gifts equal to approximately 4% of the market value of the Fund. Roughly half this money is designated for current use and half for endowment capital purposes.

The Fund represents virtually all the assets of the University less plant and equipment, and it is uniquely structured such that the receipts and disbursements of all University cash flows pass through the single endowment fund, thus minimizing operating balances and liquidity reserves.

As the unsuccessful plaintiff in the original "Prudent Man" case in 1830, Harvard remains sensitive to the fiduciary nature of the task of managing the Fund. The principal element of the "Prudent Man" Rule is summarized in Scott on Trusts, § 227, as follows:

"The only general rule which can be laid down as to investments is that the trustee is under a duty to make such investments as a prudent man would make of his own property having primarily in view the preservation of the estate and the amount and regularity of the income to be derived. In various forms this rule has been stated in innumerable cases. It involves three elements, namely care and skill and caution. The trustee must exercise a reasonable degree of care in selecting investments. He must exercise a reasonable degree of skill in making the selection. He must in addition, exercise the caution which a prudent man would exercise where a primary consideration is the preservation of funds invested."

The objective of the Harvard Fund is to invest in such a manner as to create a stream of investment returns which treats equitably, in inflation adjusted dollars, all generations of students and the public as beneficiaries of the various Harvard programs, and does so at a level of risk which is prudent. Harvard's investment horizon must consider current needs as well as the needs of one hundred years from now. In this important respect its objective must be distinguished from objectives of funds which are investing assets to provide for a future liability many years away and from objectives of annuitants who are currently consuming benefits of investments in prior periods. Harvard must effectively balance current returns and future returns. It is hoped that a level of current return can be realized which will allow for a spending rate of 4% to 5% of current market value (depending on the period in the market cycle) to support annual operating expenses.

The goal for long-term appreciation of principal is a rate such that the level of spending from the current return can be maintained in constant dollars. If this return can be achieved, the University can function in a stable environment. The annual inflow of gifts to capital, which it is hoped will continue to be roughly 2% of market value, will provide necessary capital for real growth. The 4% to 5% of current market value spent annually will be generated each year in interest and dividend income. This relatively high current yield requirement means that fixed income securities, as well as equities, will probably always be part of the investment approach. In addition, it is hoped that the appreciation of the underlying principal can be achieved with as little risk or market volatility as possible. Although capital markets do not function smoothly or predictably, Harvard's investment-return needs can be characterized as falling within a rather narrow "comfort zone." If the long-term rate of growth, assuming a 4 to 5 percent layout, is less than the inflation rate, then the Fund's contribution to the budget will have to shrink with an unacceptable amount coming from tuition, fees and other sources, or the University will have to reduce its operating budget. Conversely, while exceeding the investment objective would be nice, it should not be done by taking excessive risk or injecting greater volatility.

To implement its investment objective, Harvard has created a unique investment management structure. The Harvard Management Company was formed to be the University's principal investment adviser and will serve only the University's accounts. This group will be supplemented by five external advisers, each of which will initially manage twenty-five million dollars as well as providing specified investment research and advice with respect to the HMC portfolio. Each outside adviser has a specific set of investment objectives as well as objectives with respect to its relationship to the Harvard Management Company.

An investment strategy has been developed as a means of working towards the achievement of the investment objectives. The following disciplines are part of this strategy:

1. Under present and foreseeable market conditions, the portfolio should maintain an equity ratio of no more than 75% of assets and no less than 40%.
2. In those years when an excess of income is earned over the

targeted amount, the University intends that incremental income will not be "paid out" but will be reserved so that the "lean" income years can be subsidized. From the University's point of view, it should be able to count on a consistent, predictable income stream. Unfortunately, the market is not consistent or predictable and, therefore, a "smoothing" approach must be undertaken.

The debt/equity ratio, therefore, assumes a double purpose:

(a) to balance the needs of the University for growth in income and asset value with the existing opportunities/risks of the bond and equity markets; and

(b) to minimize market volatility or risk.

There are a number of investment approaches by which a given objective can be accomplished. Historically a basically consistent approach has tended to yield better long-term results than a style which is essentially opportunistic. It is also important that a given investment approach fit the individual style of the personnel making the investment decisions. Within this framework, the Harvard portfolio will utilize the following concepts:

1. A long-term investment horizon supported by a considerable amount of patience. Timing is a fallible art at best. A long enough time horizon, however, helps to diminish the vagaries of faulty timing.

2. A high standard of quality both in individual issues as well as in the portfolio as a whole. Investments in lesser quality should be minimized in the overall portfolio. Quality will be defined by past demonstrated results combined with a reasonable projection of continued success in the future.

3. A realization that asset allocation within prescribed limits between equities and fixed-income securities must be reviewed throughout market cycles.

4. A research approach that emphasizes macroeconomic analysis, political and social conditions, and sector economic patterns as well as individual company research.

5. In the equity portion of the portfolio, heavy emphasis will be placed on successful corporations. Such corporations have similar characteristics:

   (a) strong unit growth rates, either from superior marketing, new product introduction or a large asset base.

   (b) strong pricing flexibility due to differentiated products or favorable supply and demand characteristics.

   (c) favorable cost structure derived from low labor costs, favorable raw material cost, or efficient marketing and manufacturing operations

   (d) strong financial resources coupled with a high return on equity.

   (e) a management team in depth which is able to reflect a
      clear and understandable corporate image.
6. A lower than average turnover ratio which will reflect a
   combination of a long term horizon with correct stock selection.
7.   A fully diversified portfolio with representation of quality
   companies from all sectors of the economy.
8. A portfolio beta no greater than 1.0.
9. A bond portfolio strategy which will emphasize maturity
   and selection using higher quality, marketable debt instruments.

March 5, 1975

3. CUSTODIANSHIP AND BANK RELATIONS

As most trustees know, cash balances are a valuable commodity. So, at the very least, the trustees, or the investment committee, should know just what the institution's cash balances are. These balances include not only the institution's bank accounts and short-term investments but *all* funds held by others which can and should be made available to the institution. Once the balances properly belonging to the institution have been identified, the investment committee can decide what to do with them. One use, of course, is to make them available to a bank in the form of non-interest-bearing accounts. This use can be regarded as payment for bank services, but the investment committee should be satisfied that the value of the balances is no greater than the value of the services received.

A decade and more ago, when interest rates were low, financial managers in colleges and universities as well as in businesses were rather casual about leaving substantial cash balances in non-interest-bearing commercial checking accounts. In return, a variety of services, including the processing of checks, were usually provided to the depositor. But there was rather little analysis, on the part of either bank or depositor, of the true value of the balances and the true cost of the services rendered.

As interest rates began to rise in the late 1960s, corporate treasurers began to realize that they were losing money by keeping balances in non-interest-paying accounts when they could invest the money in treasury bills; commercial paper; certificates of deposit; or other short-term, interest-paying, money market instruments. As the amounts maintained in non-interest-paying accounts began to decline, bankers were unenthusiastic but generally cooperative about working out with corporate treasurers the value of the services rendered by the bank and the level of balances that constituted "fair" payment for the services. Colleges and universities were generally slower than businesses to tighten up on nonearning cash balances

161

(some observers attribute this to the presence of representatives of the institutions' banks on their boards of trustees), but by the late 1960s, at least some colleges and universities were managing cash efficiently. And in recent years, a few institutions have developed controls over cash balances and collections as effective as any controls one is likely to find in well-managed business corporations.

The collection of revenues is a process that is likely to offer additional opportunities for making more funds available. Promptly collecting bills is helpful; granting discounts for early payment and imposing penalties for late payment may be worthwhile. Converting a check that has been received into usable funds can often be made more efficient; an institution can sometimes invest the proceeds of a check on the same day the check is received. (Banks should give same-day credit on wire transfers, which can be used for some receipts, including withdrawals from The Common Fund for Short-Term Investments. A transfer from bank to bank by Federal Reserve wire before the 2:15 P.M. [eastern time] Federal Reserve cutoff time gives the receiving bank the use of the money on the same day.)

Sometimes funds are being held for a college or university without the institution's knowledge. The use of several banks for depositing funds, a failure to review balances daily, and reliance on the bank balances shown by the institution's books rather than by the banks' books will all contribute to ignorance of the funds that really belong to the institution but may have slipped beyond its control. It is generally a good idea to ask each bank for a monthly calculation of the institution's average daily collected balance. Not infrequently, a bank collects dividend and interest income on an institutional endowment as it comes in and remits the income to the institution at stated intervals—monthly or quarterly. The bank, of course, has the use of this income until it is remitted, and the institution may not even know what it has given up.

Once revenue has been collected and converted into usable funds as rapidly as possible, and the investment committee is satisfied that it has identified all of the institution's cash balances, including balances that the institution does not control but could control, then a decision can be made as to just what to do with those balances. Banks provide services that have to be paid for, in the form of either cash fees or non-interest-paying balances. An institution that believes it can invest those balances more profitably than its bank can will find balances an inefficient form of payment for services; Harvard, for example, maintains no balances with commercial banks. For institutions that are not in a position to invest cash balances more profitably than can their banks (or at a higher rate than their banks are willing to impute to balances), it may make good sense to pay for bank services in the form of deposits. And for a small institution a bank may be unwilling to forego balances. In these cases, however, the services and fees, as well as the credit given on balances, should be quite explicit. It is appropriate that someone carefully audit the bank relationship each year to see whether the institution is as efficient as it should be in the collection of revenue and in its use of cash balances. But the evaluation of services being received and the price being paid can hardly be carried out by trustees themselves or even by an investment committee. At some institutions, financial officers of the institution itself can perform this function. At other institutions, it is probably worth retaining the services of an accounting firm.

One of the important services a bank can render is the custodianship of investment securities. While some colleges and universities, usually those with rather small securities holdings, simply rent a safe deposit box in which they store certificates registered in the institution's name, most institutions turn the safekeeping of securities over to a bank. The securities are registered in a bank nominee name, so that the bank can accept and deliver certificates on behalf of the institution.[1] In such cases, bonded safekeeping is customary; that is, the bank carries insurance to reimburse the institution for losses due to embezzlement or mistake. Clipping of coupons and remittance of the proceeds are normally a part of the safekeeping function but may entail extra fees.

The custodian bank may also serve as a collector of income—generally dividends and interest—on the securities it holds. The common practice is to make remittances of income to the institution at stated intervals, often monthly or quarterly, which is attractive to the bank since it has the use of the income from the time of receipt to the time of remittance. At the least, the bank will prefer not to transmit income to the institution or invest it on the institution's behalf until after the bank has received it. Some institutions, however, have agreements with a custodian bank calling for the transmission of dividends and interest on the day after the dividends and interest become payable to security holders. This means that the bank takes full responsibility for collecting income on time and must bear the cost of any delays in collection.

A custodian bank can also take care of receipts and disbursements of cash on the sale and purchase of securities. And once again, the college or university can find opportunities for conserving cash and putting it to work. Usually a bank will effect the cash payments or credit cash receipts to the institution on the official settlement date of the transaction or the day after the official settlement date. But since a seller's broker is sometimes unable to produce certificates on the official settlement date and is not entitled to payment before delivery, the institution's bank will hold the cash payment on these "fails to deliver" until delivery is finally made. But the bank will usually charge the institution's account on the settlement date. During this time, of course, the institution is entitled to all dividends or interest on the purchased securities, but it will have given the use of the unpaid purchase price to the bank. An alert institution will insist on having the use of this balance.

Some finer points in sales and purchases concern dividend overpayments and dividends due on purchased securities. Dividend overpayments result from sales of securities after the dividend record date but before the ex-dividend date (the date up to which the purchaser, rather than the seller, is entitled to the dividend). As a result, the selling institution will actually receive the dividend but will owe it to the purchaser. The custodian bank can be instructed to wait until it is actually billed for this dividend before charging it against the institution. On the other side, the institution may purchase a security after the record date but before the ex-dividend date, so that the dividend has to be collected from the seller or the seller's broker. In this case, the institution's arrangement with its custodian bank can call for the institution to be credited automatically on the day following the dividend payment date, and the bank will protect itself by refusing to accept the delivery of the certificates from the seller's broker without an accompanying due bill from the broker (in effect a check for the dividend payable on the day the dividend is payable).

A certain amount of record keeping by the bank will have to accompany even the basic safekeeping function. This would include, for example, a record of all vault activity. But the custodian bank may also be in an excellent position to do quite substantial record keeping, right through to complete investment performance measurement. A bank that is handling purchases and sales, as well as all income collection (and, of course, such things as stock splits and stock dividends), has all the essential data at hand. The ability of the bank to process data accurately and provide promptly the records and reports needed by the institution and its investment committee may be an important factor in selecting a custodian.

Selecting a custodian calls for a careful comparison of costs, services, and quality of service among candidates. The best assurance that the present custodial fees and services are appropriate, of course, will come from some "shopping around." The bank and custodial arrangements and the level of efficiency in an institution's handling of cash call for regular evaluation. The sums of money at stake can be quite substantial compared with the income on the endowment.

4. SHORT-TERM INVESTMENTS

At least a portion of most college and university endowment funds is likely to be invested from time to time in short-term securities—treasury bills, certificates of deposit, and the like. Short-term investments generally serve as a source of liquidity. They may reflect anticipated withdrawals or expenditure or anticipated investments in longer-term securities when the time is appropriate. Occasionally, endowment funds may be invested in short-term securities because the manager believes that these are more profitable than longer-term alternatives. In the long run, one would expect long-term securities to offer a greater rate of return than short-term securities, so a manager who seeks a high rate of return in short-term securities is betting on his ability to forecast moves in the securities markets generally. On other occasions, short-term investments simply constitute a buying reserve to take care of unexpected and unusual opportunities to purchase stocks.

The Nature of Short-Term Balances

For most institutions, the bulk of short-term investments will represent not endowment funds but simply working capital—temporary cash surpluses from tuition and fees or government appropriations or from gifts or grants that must be invested pending expenditure for designated purposes. For institutions with large enrollments and small endowments, the short-term cash balance may be much larger than the endowment, and the investment performance of short-term funds will be more important than that of endowment. This is a point that sometimes escapes trustees.

Most institutions show a seasonal pattern in their cash flows. A research study sponsored by The Common Fund in 1972 indicated that, for the 55 institutions participating in the study, August and September generally showed substantial cash inflows; November and December showed substantial outflows; January showed again sub-

stantial inflows; and April, May, and June were months of large outflows. This seasonal fluctuation was more substantial for private
institutions than it was for public institutions. And as one might expect,
small institutions showed greater fluctuation in cash flows than did
large institutions. Indeed, some large institutions showed very little
fluctuation.

In 1972, The Common Fund undertook to find out the approximate magnitude of cash balances and short-term investments for
colleges and universities, the manner in which the investments were
being made, and the possibility of significantly improving the investment performance of short-term funds through the use of a pooled
portfolio, somewhat analogous to The Common Fund's pool of regular endowment funds. It was not possible to gather much information
on the actual investment performance record of short-term funds,
since very few institutions measure the performance of their short-
term investments or even have available data from which measurements could be made. (Virtually none of the 55 institutions surveyed
had any idea of the rate of return it had achieved on its short-
term funds, although a few had the accounting records necessary to
determine the rate.) But it was possible to find out in general how
short-term funds were being managed.

Management of Short-Term Investments

At most colleges and universities, the management of short-term
investments was a part-time responsibility of the institution's chief
financial officer or one of his assistants. Investment advice might
come from banks or securities dealers, but usually it was limited to
selection of securities available for a specific maturity. Short-term
securities were almost always held to maturity, and the maturities
were chosen to meet anticipated needs. Small institutions as well as
some large universities with quite substantial cash balances and short-
term investments followed this policy, and it suggests some serious
limitations on potential investment performance.

First, the practice of holding all short-term investments to maturity, and therefore having to specify maturities of all securities to fit
anticipated cash needs, limits the range of possible investment and
completely ignores the state of the money market and rates available
on instruments of different maturities. (Institutions that manage their
short-term portfolios, changing maturities to match interest rate expectations, seem to achieve higher rates of return.) Second, institutions that follow this policy may be holding larger nonearning bank

balances than they should. An institution that is reluctant to sell short-term securities before maturity must maintain bank balances to meet its unexpected needs for cash. Third, failure or inability to make use of professional money market managers for short-term invest- ments may deprive the institution of the higher returns that skillful management might achieve.

An institution can do a number of things to improve the perfor- mance of its short-term funds. First, it can minimize its nonearning bank balances. Probably few institutions today are unaware of the benefits of shifting funds from nonearning bank balances into profit- able money market instruments. As far back as 1968, some colleges and universities were working hard to cut their bank balances to a minimum and to invest as much as possible in short-term instruments. Concentrating bank balances, monitoring the balances carefully, es- timating the balances really necessary to compensate a bank for ser- vices, and devising ways of speeding collections and transfers may all help to keep the nonearning balances at a minimum.

The next step is to improve the investment management itself. The high short-term interest rates of the last couple of years have led to the emergence of a number of liquid-asset mutual funds. These funds offer opportunities for quick deposit and withdrawal, diversifi- cation among money market instruments, and professional manage- ment. Whether or not the quality of management makes a difference, the other advantages are probably enough to recommend these funds to institutions with small excess cash balances.

Another alternative for institutions with respectable balances is a master note arrangement. This consists of a sort of miniature diver- sified fund, with a bank acting within the terms of a single note to invest institutional funds in corporate commercial paper such that, within specified limits, the corporate issuers will immediately issue new paper as the institution has funds to invest or redeem paper if the institution has a need for cash.

Finally, The Common Fund has developed a pooled short-term fund for colleges and universities.

Performance of Short-Term Funds

The research sponsored by The Common Fund, drawing on the performance records of the very few institutions that keep such rec- ords of short-term investment and comparing them with the per- formance records of large, professionally managed short-term pools, suggested that the pooling device might add from 1 to 3 percent in rate of return beyond what the individual institutions could do for themselves.[1] A pooled fund should achieve superior performance for a number of reasons.

A pooled short-term fund is inherently more stable than the short-term investments of individual institutions. The Common Fund's research indicated that a pool of the short-term investments of 55 institutions would fluctuate in size substantially less than would the short-term investments of the average individual institution. Also, the fluctuations of the pool are easier to predict than are those of the investments of an individual institution. Hence, the pool can afford to invest in longer maturities than can the individual institutions and can plan the turnover of its portfolio better than the individual institutions can. A pool also offers some advantages of scale in purchasing and selling securities, in obtaining the services of good professional managers, and in diversification of portfolio securities.

The Common Fund's research also indicated that institutions participating in a pooled fund, from which they could make immediate cash withdrawals on virtually no notice, could afford to maintain lower nonearning cash balances and to put more of their unused funds into short-term investments.

The Common Fund for Short-Term Investment

As a result of the research, The Common Fund trustees decided that a pooled fund for short-term investments of colleges and universities should be established. And in September 1974 the fund was launched—The Common Fund for Short-Term Investments, organized as a common trust fund under the federal banking laws. A committee of the trustees of The Common Fund provide continuing advice on investment policy and monitor investment results. In early 1975, the fund size was about $50 million.

5. SECURITY LENDING

Brokers often need to borrow stocks and bonds for the purpose of making delivery on short sales or for covering "fails." The benefit to an institution that lends securities lies in the cash collateral that the broker posts for the full market value of the securities he borrows; the lender can invest this cash in short-term securities. In addition, the borrower pays the lender the dividends or interest on the securities he has borrowed.

Properly handled, bond and stock lending appears to offer almost no risk. Of course, the institution must be sure that collateral is maintained at full market value on a day-to-day basis. But the institution lends the bonds or stocks on a day-to-day basis and can usually call them in at any time. The interest or dividends are somewhat at risk because they are not protected by collateral and because the broker who arranged the loan could become insolvent. But this risk, at worst, seems very small and can be minimized by careful selection of the brokers and the custodian bank. In general, the key to minimal risk is very careful arrangements.

A survey of the member institutions of the National Association of College and University Business Officers as of June 30, 1974, indicated that of 131 respondents 44 percent had not considered lending securities, 11 percent were considering lending, 21 percent had rejected lending, and 24 percent were lending. But of the 26 institutions with endowments over $65 million, 20 were lending securities, and only 2 had rejected the practice.

Profitability

The gross proceeds of stock lending consist of the interest earned on short-term investments. In 1973 and 1974, when interest rates were high, brokers were able to extract rebates from lenders in the form of a portion of this interest. When short-term rates were around 12 percent, brokers were demanding 3.5 percent, leaving 8.5 percent for the lender. As interest rates dropped to 5.5 percent, the brokers reduced their demands to 2.5 percent, leaving only 3 percent for the lender.

Some lenders use "finders" to place security loans, and the usual finder's fee of 1 percent further reduces the profitability of security lending.

Costs of lending include the custodian's transaction fee, which ranges from about $10 to $25 per transaction (with two transactions needed to complete a loan and its repayment), and additional costs if the custodian handles the lending arrangements. Most institutions that engage in security lending also incur internal administrative costs.

The following equation may help an institution to determine whether it can profitably lend securities:

(percent of short-term interest rate − percent of finder's fee and rebate)

$$\times \text{(loan amount)} \times \frac{\text{days loan outstanding}}{365} - \text{(2 transaction costs)}$$

− (institutional overhead per loan) = profit on loan.

From this equation it is possible to estimate, for prevailing interest-rate and cost conditions, the level of loans necessary to break even. A plausible set of conditions in mid-1975 might be represented by:

$$\text{(5.5 percent − 2.5 percent)} \times \text{(loan amount)} \times \frac{\text{days loan outstanding}}{365}$$

$$- (2 \times \$15) - \$10 = 0$$

loan amount × days loan outstanding = $487,000

Under these conditions (an internal cost figure of $10 per loan assumes a fairly high volume), the product of the loan amount and the days outstanding would have to be nearly 500,000. This could be represented by a $100,000 loan outstanding for five days, for example, or a $250,000 loan outstanding for two days. Anything less would lead to a loss. Five days is probably longer than the average life of a security loan.

It is critical that an institution contemplating security lending have a cost accounting system that accurately identifies the expenses of a lending program. Indeed, there is evidence that some of the institutions that made large incomes from stock lending on the high interest rates of 1974 may have lost money in 1975 without realizing what happened.

But security lending is not dependent on high interest rates. Of the 32 institutions that reported lending endowment securities, fewer began lending in 1973 or 1974 than began in 1971 or 1972, when rates were much lower.[1]

6. REAL ESTATE EQUITIES

A hundred years ago or more, college and university endowment funds were substantially invested in mortgages and real estate equity holdings. But in the early 1900s, particularly the 1920s, endowment funds began to abandon mortgages and real estate and to move substantially into common stocks. Today, few colleges and universities have significant mortgage portfolios or investments in income-producing real estate, although a number, of course, have substantial real estate holdings, largely for protection and future expansion.

In the 1970s, the stock market has proved disappointing, inflation is high, and there is widespread interest in a possible return to the land. Investment committees have begun to ask whether real estate is an appropriate investment vehicle for endowment funds, and if so, just how they should proceed.

The Apparent Benefit of Real Estate Investment

Real estate offers an obvious device for diversifying equity investments beyond common stocks, although it is not demonstrably more profitable than investment in common stocks. No statistics on real estate values over a long period of time analogous to the stock market indexes are available as a basis for profitability conclusions. Various studies of trends in real estate values are available, but none are representative of diversified real estate portfolios. The history of the real estate investment trusts (REITs) is short and mixed; many have shown disastrous results over the last year or so. In 1974, pension funds polled by Money Market Directories Inc., seemed to *expect* an income yield of 8 to 10 percent and an appreciation of 2 to 4 percent on real estate, probably not very different from common stock expectations.[1]

The real estate market may be less efficient than the stock market in the sense that it offers opportunities for unusually high rates of return through astute management which probably do not exist in the stock market. It is also possible that the 1974 Pension Reform Act's encouragement of diversification may lead increasing numbers of pension funds into the real estate area (where some are beginning to be invested already) and raise the prices of the kinds of real estate that lend themselves to institutional investment.

Tax Problems and Unrelated Business Income

A normally tax-exempt endowment fund can generate "unrelated business income," which is subject to federal income tax if it incurs debt in the acquisition of investment assets or if it enters the conduct of an active business.[2] Fortunately, rent is treated under the Internal Revenue Code as "passive" income, and, generally speaking, activities that simply generate rent are not considered to be the conduct of an active business. But many kinds of real estate investment may well involve an active business.

The generation of unrelated business income is not necessarily bad. The after-tax return on an unrelated business venture may be as high as the tax-free return from an exempt activity of about the same risk. In computing taxable income from an unrelated business, an endowment fund is entitled to deduct expenses such as depreciation (only straight-line depreciation and only in proportion to the fraction of income that is unrelated business income), and losses from one unrelated business may be offset by profits from another. In any case, many devices are available to enable an endowment fund to participate in real estate investments without engaging in an unrelated business.

Leases may be used to convert profits from an active business into passive income. Similarly, the use of leases can make it possible for an endowment fund to participate in a real estate venture that involves the use of debt without the endowment fund itself borrowing to make an acquisition and involving itself in an unrelated business. For example, an endowment fund could purchase land, without incurring any debt, and then lease the land to a developer who will construct an improvement, perhaps with borrowed money. The developer's debt does not turn the endowment investment into an unrelated business.

These arrangements may be quite complex and require very careful planning by lawyers familiar with all the intricacies of the taxation of charitable funds. They are not inexpensive, and the highly specialized talent they require may put them beyond the reach of many institutions that are unable to make quite substantial commitments to real estate.

Risks and Costs

The real estate market is an equity market, and, like any equity market, it involves the risk of losing money. In addition, making a profit in real estate seems to demand very able and very aggressive managers; the kind of passive investment that may secure adequate although not impressive returns in the stock market will probably fail to obtain even adequate returns in the real estate market. Nevertheless, there are those who believe that real estate equities are less volatile than common stocks. This proposition is difficult to test because it is extremely difficult to obtain reliable market valuations of real estate held in a portfolio. Hopes for a low volatility may be founded more on the opportunities for *reporting* stable values for real estate than on the belief that true values are really stable. Stability is, of course, enhanced if the real estate investment is unleveraged by debt. Debt-free real estate ownership, very unusual for tax-paying investors, is not unusual for tax-exempt investors.

Real estate offers some risk beyond the chance of losing money. The common stock investment program of an endowment fund has social implications, but these implications become much more significant in a real estate program. Particularly if the academic side of an institution is concerned with land-use planning, urban renewal, and solutions for the nation's housing problems, structuring a real estate portfolio so as not to run into conflict with various constituencies in the institution may be quite difficult. And real estate investment may well create opportunities for groups outside the institution to voice criticism on social and political grounds.

Some universities already have substantial experience in the legal and the tax-planning aspects of a real estate program because they are already involved in real estate investment and perhaps in development around their own campuses. These institutions may also have the expert management that is difficult to find and expensive when it can be found. Management fees may be 1 percent of a substantial real estate portfolio (for *portfolio* management, not *property* management); they would probably be under 0.5 percent for a common stock portfolio of comparable size. Given the substantial cost of developing individual real estate investments for an endowment fund and the need for diversification to reduce risk, unless the endowment is prepared to commit around $100 million to real estate, this avenue is not practical. An alternative is the purchase of an interest in a pool of real estate assets.

Pooled Real Estate Funds

There are, of course, plenty of publicly owned REITs. In early 1975, the units in most of these trusts were selling far below their prices of a year or two ago. Many would therefore argue that now is the time to invest and pick up real estate interests at greatly depressed prices. But the general reputation of the REIT industry is such that probably few college or university investment committees would feel comfortable investing in it. No pooled funds presently seem to be available to endowment funds, although some are available to pension funds and their reports may be of interest to institutions considering the possibility of forming a pooled fund. Among these are Fund F of the First National Bank of Chicago and PRISA of the Prudential Insurance Company of America.

The former was established in 1973, and by November 30, 1974, had assets of $63 million (represented by 12 properties in 12 cities and 7 states) and 35 participating retirement trusts. Fund F is exempt from federal income tax and entirely unleveraged; its long-run diversification target, as of early 1975, was 35 percent residential, 20 percent office, 20 percent industrial, 15 percent retail, and 10 percent land. (The fund's policy is *not* to invest in mortgages, partnerships, development positions, hotels, and long-term fixed positions without escalation provisions and ground leases.) The fund is managed by the Real Estate Investment Division of the First National Bank of Chicago Trust Department in conjunction with the bank's subsidiary Real Estate Research Corporation. Participating retirement trusts may enter the fund once a month by purchasing units.

PRISA was established in 1970, and by September 30, 1974, had assets of $537 million (represented by 160 properties, 4 partnership positions, $40 million in mortgage loans, and almost $100 million in short-term investments) and 104 participating pension funds. PRISA is leveraged, and as of September 30, 1974, its property investments were: 13 percent apartments, 24 percent offices, 32 percent industrial, 16 percent commercial, 14 percent hotels and motels, 0.3 percent land under lease, and 0.3 percent farms. The fund is managed by the real estate department of the Prudential Insurance Company. Investments in PRISA by participating pension funds must be individually arranged to fit PRISA's needs.

For the most part, an investment in a pooled fund is illiquid and not very marketable. Some of the funds do have redemption provisions, although redemption seems to be dependent upon the fund's cash flow, which is not entirely certain. Some have limited lives and offer the prospect of a complete payout within a specified time period. But again, the ability of the fund to meet this payout is not certain. Although investment in one of these funds does not require the substantial management and legal preparations that an institution must make to engage in real estate development on its own, still a careful legal analysis is appropriate to make sure that there are no unexpected tax consequences. Also, in general, the management fees for these funds are high compared to the fees paid to managers of common stock funds. Use of the fund, of course, may still expose the institution to some social and political risks, depending upon the particular developments the fund undertakes.

As yet, the choice of pooled real estate funds is rather restricted and appears to be limited to participation by pension funds. Presumably, a number of banks and insurance companies have the expertise needed to put together pooled funds. And colleges and universities clearly are becoming more interested in real estate investments. The combination may serve to make pooled funds available.

7. WRITING CALL OPTIONS

Put and call options have been available as investment vehicles for many years. But institutional investors have tended to regard them as highly speculative devices,[1] and until recently, there was no well-organized market for trading in options. The establishment of the Chicago Board Options Exchange (CBOE), in April 1973, presented institutions for the first time with an auction market and visible prices. Dealings in options began to gain in respectability. Perhaps for this reason, or perhaps simply because of the stock market's decline in recent years, more institutions seem to have become aware that selling call options is a defensive investment strategy that may reduce the risk in a common stock portfolio.

In January 1975, the American Stock Exchange initiated trading in call options, and as of June 1975, call options on 58 common stocks are traded on the CBOE, while options on another 30 stocks are traded on the American Exchange. Neither exchange so far provides a market for put options.

The Call Option

A call option is a contract entitling its holder to purchase 100 shares of the underlying (optioned) stock at the stated exercise price, or "striking" price, at any time prior to the expiration date of the option. The seller or "writer" of the option may then be called upon to deliver 100 shares of the optioned stock, at the exercise price, at any time prior to expiration of the option.

From the option buyer's point of view, an option offers the opportunity to speculate in a common stock with a relatively small dollar commitment. For example, on April 15, 1975, the common stock of IBM closed at $209½. The October 200 option closed at $27. So an investor either could have purchased 100 shares of IBM for a total of $20,950; or he could have purchased an option on 100 shares of IBM, at an exercise price of $200 per share, expiring on October 27, 1975, for a total of $2,700 (apart from brokerage costs in each case). In both cases, the investor benefits from an increase in the price of IBM shares. But the potential rate of return on the option is much greater than the potential on the purchase of the stock itself. If IBM were to rise to $250 per share by October 27, the purchaser of the 100 shares would have made $4,050 on a $20,950 investment (apart from dividends), or about 19.3 percent. At a stock price of $250 per share, the option would be worth $5,000 (the difference between the $200 per share at which the investor can buy the stock and the $250 market value of the stock), and the buyer of the option would have made $2,300 on a $2,700 investment (again apart from brokerage costs), or about 85 percent. But the option purchase is also very risky. If IBM were to decline to less than $200 per share on October 27, the option would become worthless, and the option buyer would have suffered a 100 percent loss.

The buying of call options can be carried on in a less speculative manner. But it is unlikely that purchasing call options will appeal to college and university investment committees as a prudent investment strategy. The *writing* of call options, particularly covered call options, on the other hand can be a very conservative strategy.

Writing Call Options

Consider an institution that owns 100 shares of IBM, worth $20,950, in early 1975. By selling the October 200 option for a total of $2,700, the institution limits its opportunity to profit from a substantial price rise in IBM but also reduces the potential loss from a price decline. If the price should rise to $250 on October 27—indeed, if it should rise to any level above $200—the 100 shares of stock will be called, and the institution will sell those share at $200. The $20,000 proceeds of sale, plus the $2,700 from the sale of the call option, represent a gain of $1,750 over the initial investment of $20,950 (apart from dividends), for a return of about 8.4 percent over six and a half months, corresponding to about 15.4 percent per year (again ignoring brokerage costs). This is the most the institution can make as long as IBM stock reaches at least $200 on October 27. If the price is below $200 on that date, the institution will make less.

If the stock price were to fall to $190 on October 27, the option would not be exercised and the institution would be left with 100 shares worth a total of $19,000 and the $2,700 proceeds of the sale of the call option. The 9.3 percent decline in the value of the stock would be more than offset by the proceeds of the sale of the option, and the rate of return would be 3.6 percent, corresponding to 6.6 percent per year (again apart from dividends and ignoring brokerage costs). Since the call option was sold for $2,700—that is, at $27 per share—the price of the stock can drop $27 from $209.50, to $182.50, before the institution loses money on the combination of ownership of 100 shares and sale of a call option. Should the price fall below $182.50, the institution will lose, but it will not lose as much as it would have lost had it not sold the call option.

The transaction described above is the sale of a "covered" option. That is, the institution writing the option held the optioned shares throughout the life of the option and was prepared to deliver them at the exercise price. It is also possible to write uncovered or "naked" options. In this case, the institution does not hold the optioned shares. In the event that the call option is exercised, the institution will have to purchase the shares in the market and deliver them at the exercise price. (So-called variable hedging involves the sale of both covered and naked options.) The sale of naked options is very similar to the short sale of stock and has all the risks of short selling. Short selling and the sale of naked options are not necessarily inappropriate for an endowment fund. Through careful handling of sales and covering, reliable managers and brokers can hold risk of loss to predetermined levels. But few institutions are likely to feel that the activity is prudent.

The Call Option Market

Before April 19, 1973, all options were purchased and written on an over-the-counter basis through brokers working with a put and call broker. Each contract was individually arranged between a writer and a purchaser, and contracts were not uniform in their terms. As a result, the market was not very liquid, prices were not openly displayed, and the writer of an option could end his obligation under that option only by negotiating with the buyer of the same option. Today there is still a minor over-the-counter market in call options, but the CBOE and the AMEX markets offer substantially improved trading conditions, standardized contracts, and liquidity, although options on only 88 stocks (at the time of writing) are traded in these markets.

Both the CBOE and the AMEX operate continuous auction markets. An investor can learn the bid and ask price on an option as easily as he can learn the bid and ask price on a listed stock. Quotations are shown on brokers' desk top displays and in many newspapers. And these markets offer liquidity similar to the liquidity that can be found on the stock exchanges. Writers and buyers of call options are not matched in these markets. The writer of a call option—an IBM October 200 option, for example—can eliminate his liability under an outstanding option simply by purchasing such an option. His obligation on the option he wrote is exactly canceled out by his entitlement under the option he has purchased, because contracts in both markets are standardized. All contracts involve 100 shares of the underlying common stock. Expiration dates are uniform; expiration for options in any particular stock is always on the last Monday of one of four months. Initially, the four months were January, April, July, and October for all stocks. But the exchanges are forming 3 groups of listed options and will use all 12 months for expirations. At any one time, options are available in the closest three of these months. So on April 15, 1975, options were available on IBM stock expiring on April 28, July 28, and October 27. The exercise price is set by the exchange, close to the market price of the underlying stock. As the price of the stock changes, additional options may be authorized at different exercise prices. For example, as of April 15, 1975, options on IBM stock were available for April, July, and October, at exercise prices of 220, 200, 180, and 160, for a total of 12 different IBM options, offering a variety of levels of downside protection and upside potential.

As a practical matter, an option writer can generally avoid having stocks called away from him simply by repurchasing his call option. For example, suppose an institution has sold an IBM October 200 option, and the price of IBM rises to 0250 a share. The price of the option will be at least $50, because the holder of the option is entitled to purchase IBM at $200 a share and can sell it at $250 a share. (The "intrinsic value" of the option is $50.) The option will probably sell at a little more than $50 a share, with the excess above $50 representing the advantages of holding an option good until October 27—the "time value" of the option. The holder of such an option who wishes to realize his profit is not likely to exercise his right to buy the stock. Because of transaction costs, he is more likely to sell the option. So no matter how high the price of IBM stock goes, an October 200 option probably will not be exercised until close to October 27, unless it happens to sell at or below intrinsic value, so that arbitraging becomes profitable. The writer of an option who sees the stock price rising and does not wish to have his stock called away from him can always repurchase the call option himself. This is a "closing purchase," and the result is not the acquisition of a new call option but the cancelation of the obligation under the original option. Of course the option writer may pay in the closing purchase more than he received for the option he sold. And to the extent that the option price still reflects time value, he will be a little worse off in terms of dollars than if he had permitted the stock to be called away from him.

If the stock price on October 27 is above $200, then all the October contracts outstanding on that date will be exercised. And probably some contracts will have been exercised before October 27. (Exercise becomes fairly likely about two weeks before the expiration date.) The exercise of an option takes place through the Options Clearing Corporation, and the Clearing Corporation selects at random a writer of the October 200 contract, calling upon that writer to deliver the 100 shares of the underlying stock at a price of $200 per share. At this point, it is no longer possible for the writer to make a closing purchase and avoid the need to deliver shares of stock. But he may purchase another 100 shares of stock on the market and deliver these shares under the option.

Taxes and Unrelated Business Income

The proceeds of sale of a call option are not considered a dividend or interest or gain from the sale or exchange of a security. If the call is unexercised, the proceeds to a college or university constitute unrelated business income, which is of course taxable.[2] If the stock price rises sufficiently and the call is exercised, the proceeds of sale of the call are treated as part of the proceeds of sale of the stock and therefore part of a capital gain (or reduction of loss), and they are not taxable. But if the institution repurchases the call option in order to nullify its obligation under the option it has written, any loss on the option will be an unrelated business loss, which can be used to offset unrelated business income. For example, if an institution has sold an IBM October 200 contract at a price of $27, for a total of $2,700, and the price of the stock rises to $250, then the price of the October 200 contract will rise to approximately $50, and the institution can anticipate that, unless the stock price drops before October 27, the option will be exercised and the stock will be called. To preclude a call, the institution could purchase an October 200 contract at a price of perhaps $52, for a total of $5,200. The $2,500 loss ($5,200 minus $2,700) on the option transactions will be considered negative unrelated business income and can be used for tax purposes to offset $2,500 of unrelated business income from another transaction. The institution can even remain in an optioned position, if it wishes, by selling another option, perhaps as January 250, at the same time it repurchases the October 200.

As of early 1975, a bill has been introduced in Congress to remove option-writing income altogether from unrelated business income.

Option-Writing Strategies for an Endowment Fund

The writing of covered call options is a conservative strategy that can be used solely as a device for reducing downside risk in a common stock investment, although of course it also limits the upside potential.

But an institution can reduce risk in other ways, for example, by committing a portion of its assets to common stock and investing the balance in long-term bonds or money market instruments. The question then is whether the sale of call options is a better way to reduce risk.

There is evidence that at least until recently, the call option market offered an unusually profitable way to reduce risk. The purchasers of call options have simply paid too much, as a general rule, for their options. And the writers of call options have benefited. But the openness of the CBOE and AMEX markets and the substantial analytic effort that is being made by investors or on their behalf may make the option market somewhat more efficient; the writers of call options may not be able to count on buyers paying excessive prices indefinitely.

But call option writing can be attractive even if the options are not overpriced. Even at "correct" prices (and correctness always involves a matter of judgment, although most option experts have mathematical formulas by which to calculate their correct or "actuarial" values for options), writing options can lead to a risk-return combination that is more attractive than the combinations available from portfolios of stocks or stocks and bonds.

Institutions may engage in writing covered call options on any of several levels. One is more or less "dabbling" with options, writing them on a casual basis on stocks held in a conventional stock portfolio. This strategy is at best dubious, in part because success or failure is almost impossible to measure. Usually, the casual writing of options is aimed at providing downside protection for the most volatile stocks and leaves the least volatile unoptioned. Black and Scholes, in testing their model for the valuation of call options—the most complete model published to date—concluded that, over the period 1966–69, the over-the-counter market had tended to put too low a price on the options for very volatile stocks and too high a price on options for stable stocks.[3] A manager who sought to limit the downside risk on volatile stocks by writing call options but did not feel it necessary to write options on stable stocks would probably have sacrificed too much potential return for the reduction in downside risk. Of course, conclusions based on data for 1966–69, when all trading was still over-the-counter, are not necessarily true of today's trading.

A second strategy has one manager concentrate on maintaining a diversified and profitable stock portfolio while a second manager—an options expert—writes options on this portfolio. Once again, it is next to impossible to measure separately the successes of the option program and the stock purchase program. And in this case, the stock manager may choose stocks that are not necessarily good option candidates, while the option manager may force the stock manager to hold the stocks on which he has written options until the options expire.

On a third level, option writing may become one of the duties of a stock portfolio manager who has little interest or expertise in option writing and whose performance in this area will probably be undistinguished.

If he is skilled and enthusiastic, we have a fourth strategy, by which the manager may combine option writing with more or less conventional stock portfolio management, selecting stocks about which he is most optimistic, with regard for diversification and perhaps for his expectations of the market as a whole. Then, once he has selected the stocks, he write options. The option writing can be careful and systematic, and the choice of options to write can be as broad as the list of stocks in the portfolio. But the option writing becomes a secondary activity, and once again it may be almost impossible to identify the specific contribution the option program has made to the overall performance of the portfolio, especially if market forecasts have played a major role in the choice of options to write. Some managers of call option programs argue that the expectation of a rising stock market calls for the sale of call options at high striking prices, providing minimum downside protection but maximum opportunity for gains and that the expectation of a declining market calls for option writing at low striking prices, for maximum downside protection and minimum opportunity for gain. The investment committee must decide whether the manager should be responsible for market forecasting and adapting the option program to these forecasts, whether the committee should rely on other sources for the forecast, or whether it should not attempt forecasting. In this last case, some policy must be established with respect to the balance between downside protection and upside potential.

The fifth strategy goes a step beyond the fourth. A portion of an institution's assets is committed to an option program, separate and distinct from the conventional stock portfolio. The manager in charge of the option program views the purchase of a stock and the simultaneous writing of a call option as a single investment. Neither the characteristics of the stock nor its qualities as an option candidate alone are enough to justify its purchase. The combination of stock purchase and option writing is what the manager must evaluate. Diversification is still important, but a market forecast is probably not.

Option writing on this level, separated from the other aspects of managing a stock portfolio, offers the best opportunity for measuring the contribution of an option program to overall performance. It also offers an opportunity for selecting an option manager solely on the strength of his expertise in option writing rather than on the basis of his overall skill in managing common stocks.

The fifth strategy has not yet been proved clearly superior to the fourth, and some institutions prefer to see option writing attached to conventional portfolio management rather than standing on its own. An investment committee, if it undertakes an option program, will have to decide which strategy it intends to follow and learn from its manager or prospective manager which strategy he intends to follow.

Spending Implications

Call option writing by endowment funds affects spending levels and growth in spending. The writing of options that are not exercised generates "income." This income is to some extent a replacement of appreciation that an unoptioned portfolio might earn. An institution that spends income yield should be aware of this conversion of appreciation into income. Unless spending is held below income, call option writing may favor current spending over future spending to an extent that the board or investment committee did not intend. An institution that spends a constant percentage of market value (this method is discussed in Chapter V) will not confront this problem, since the distinction between income yield and appreciation does not affect its spending.

8. DIVERSIFICATION REQUIREMENT UNDER THE PENSION REFORM ACT OF 1974

This statute, the Employee Retirement Income Security Act of 1974,[1] has no direct applicability to college and university endowment funds. But it is likely to have an indirect influence on the management of all trust funds and endowments. Moreover, some observers foresee federal legislation extending beyond retirement funds in the future.

Section 404 of the Act sets a standard of prudence and imposes a specific diversification requirement:

FIDUCIARY DUTIES

Section 404. (a)(1) Subject to sections 403 (c) and (d), 4042, and 4044, a fiduciary shall discharge his duties with respect to a plan solely in the interest of the participants and beneficiaries and—
  (A) for the exclusive purpose of:
    (i) providing benefits to participants and their beneficiaries; and
    (ii) defraying reasonable expenses of administering the plan;
  (B) with the care, skill, prudence, and diligence under the circumstances then prevailing that a prudent man acting in a like capacity and familiar with such matters would use in the conduct of an enterprise of a like character and with like aims;
  (C) by diversifying the investments of the plan so as to minimize the risk of large losses, unless under the circumstances it is clearly prudent not to do so. . .

The report of the Conference Committee explains the intent of the diversification requirement:[2]

Diversification requirement.—The substitute requires fiduciaries to diversify plan assets to minimize the risk of large losses, unless under the circumstances it is clearly prudent not to do so. It is not intended that a more stringent standard of prudence be established with the use of the term "clearly prudent." Instead, by using this term it is intended that in an action for plan losses based on breach of the diversification requirement, the plaintiff's initial burden will be to demonstrate that there has been a failure to diversify. The defendant then is to have the burden of demonstrating that this failure to diversify was prudent. The substitute places these relative burdens on the parties in this matter, because the basic policy is to require diversification, and if diversification on its face does not exist, then the burden of justifying failure to follow this general policy should be on the fiduciary who engages in this conduct.

The degree of investment concentration that would violate this requirement to diversify cannot be stated as a fixed percentage, because a prudent fiduciary must consider the facts and circumstances of each case. The factors to be considered include (1) the purposes of the plan; (2) the amount of the plan assets; (3) financial and industrial conditions; (4) the type of investment, whether mortgages, bonds or shares of stock or otherwise; (5) distribution as to geographical location; (6) distribution as to industries; (7) the dates of maturity.

A fiduciary usually should not invest the whole or an unreasonably large proportion of the trust property in a single security. Ordinarily the fiduciary should not invest the whole or an unduly large proportion of the trust property in one type of security or in various types of securities dependent upon the success of one enterprise or upon conditions in one locality, since the effect is to increase the risk of large losses. Thus, although the fiduciary may be authorized to invest in industrial stocks, he should not invest a disproportionate amount of the plan assets in the share of corporations engaged in a particular industry. If he is investing in mortgages on real property he should not invest a disproportionate amount of the trust in mortgages in a particular district or on a particular class of property so that a decline in property values in that district or of that class might cause a large loss.

The assets of many pension plans are managed by one or more investment managers. For example, one investment manager, A, may be responsible for 10 percent of the assets of a plan and instructed by the named fiduciary or trustee to invest solely in bonds; another investment manager, B, may be responsible for a different 10 percent of the assets of the same plan and instructed to invest solely in equities. Such arrangements often result in investment returns which are quite favorable to the plan, its participants, and its beneficiaries. In these circumstances, A would invest solely in bonds in accordance with his instructions and would diversify the bond investments in accordance with the diversification standard, the prudent man standard, and all other provisions applicable to A as a fiduciary. Similarly, B would invest solely in equities in accordance with his instructions and these standards. Neither A nor B would incur any liability for diversifying assets subject to their management in accordance with their instructions.

The conferees intend that, in general, whether the plan assets are sufficiently diversified is to be determined by examining the ultimate investment of the plan assets. For example, the conferees understand that for efficiency and economy plans may invest all their assets in a single bank or other pooled investment fund, but that the pooled fund itself could have diversified investments. It is intended that, in this case, the diversification rule is to be applied to the plan by examining the diversification of the investments in the pooled fund. The same is true with respect to investments in a mutual fund. Also, generally a plan may be invested wholly in insurance or annuity contracts without violating the diversification rules, since generally an insurance company's assets are to be invested in a diversified manner.

9. A VARIETY OF SPENDING FORMULAS

The relatively simple spending formula referred to in Chapter V may be used in averaging endowment market values over a series of years, allowing a setback for budgeting convenience and applying a spending rate to the average. This approach appears to offer all the advantages that can be found in more complex approaches; yet it is simple both to understand and to apply, and a number of institutions are using it or something close to it. But other rules are in use, and still others have been recommended.

A Simple Recommended Spending Rule

The formula is:

$$\text{Spending in fiscal year } T = S \times \left[\frac{V_{T-1} + V_{T-2} + V_{T-3} + \dots V_{T-N}}{N} \right]$$

S is the "adjusted" spending rate. V_{T-1} is the market value of the endowment fund one year before the start of the fiscal year T; V_{T-2} is the value two years before the start of the fiscal year, and so on. N is the number of years of market values to be used in the averaging.

This formula provides for a one-year setback. If the fiscal year is 1976–77, then the most recent market value to enter into the formula is V_{T-1}, the value at the end of fiscal 1974–75. This value should be known soon after the end of fiscal 1974–75 and therefore almost a year before the start of fiscal 1976–77, which allows time for fixing budgets.

The adjusted spending rate, S, is determined as follows.[1]

If r is the expected total-return rate on the endowment and g is the target growth rate, then the spending rate that should be applied to year-end market value is $r - g$. If spending is to be taken out of the endowment at the beginning of the fiscal year, then the rate to be applied to the beginning of year market value is $1 - (1 + g)/(1 + r)$.

The corresponding adjusted spending rate, to be applied to an average of N market values, with a one-year setback is:

$$S = \frac{N \times g \times [1 - (1+g)/(1+r)] \times (1+g)^N}{[(1+g)^N - 1] \times [(1+g)/(1+r)]}$$

For example, if $N = 5$ years, $g = 6$ percent, and $r = 10$ percent, then $S = 4.48$ percent.

It is a simple matter, of course, to lengthen or shorten the averaging period, by increasing or decreasing N. Changing the setback is more complicated, but it can be done.

Increasing N will lead to more stability in year-to-year spending, but it will also reduce the certainty of growth. A value of 5 for N will probably serve the needs of most institutions.

The Yale Formula[2]

The Yale spending formula may well be the first one that was developed to calculate an appropriate level of yield-plus-gain spending.

The basic formula, the "university equation," is:

$$g_{T+1} = r_T - S_T/E_T$$

where g_{T+1} is the growth rate in spending from endowment from year T to year $T + 1$, and r_T is the long-run expected total return on the endowment. S_T is actual spending from endowment in year T, and E_T is the market value of the endowment at the beginning of the year T. The spending S_T was known before the year T began. The market value E_T was known shortly after the year T began, and r_T is estimated at about the same time. So g_{T+1} is known well before the beginning of year $T + 1$, and spending in year $T + 1$, which is $(1 + g_{T+1}) \times S_T$, is also known well ahead, permitting the development of the budget for the year.

The long-run expected rate of total return, r_T, is calculated each year, on the basis of *past* performance, using a weighted-averaging process known as "exponential smoothing." The formula is:

$$1n(1 + r_T) = .8 \times 1n(1 + r_{T-1}) + .2 \times 1n(1 + a_{T-1})$$

In this formula, $1n$ is the natural logarithm, r_T is the estimated long-run rate of return to be used in calculating g_{T+1}, r_{T-1} is the estimate used the year before to calculate g_T, and a_{T+1} is the *actual* total-return rate achieved in year $T - 1$. Since r_{T-1} embodies all the actual total-return history before the year $T - 1$, then r_T is a weighted-average of both this history and the actual performance in year $T-1$. The calculation can be performed soon after the close of the year $T - 1$.

The Princeton Formula

In 1973, Professors Litvack, Malkiel, and Quandt of Princeton prepared a paper proposing a spending rule for the Princeton endowment.[3] Their formula is:

$$\text{Spending for fiscal year } T = S \times [V_{T-\frac{1}{2}} \times (1.025) + V_{T-1} \times (1.05)$$
$$+ V_{T-1\frac{1}{2}} \times (1.075) + \ldots + V_{T-3} \times (1.15)]/6$$

The quantities within the squared brackets represent a series of six semiannual market values for the endowment, set back six months before the beginning of the spending year and compounded forward to the beginning of that year at 5 percent per year. This reflects the expectation that normal growth in the endowment will be 5 percent.

The usual value for S, the spending rate, is 4 percent. This follows from an expectation that the total return on the endowment will be 9 percent and that 5 percent of this should be allocated for growth in order to offset inflation.

But the spending rate may fall below 4 percent. If a "stabilization fund" is below 50 percent of "full value," then spending is scaled down to as little as 3.2 percent, a rate corresponding to the dividend and interest yield on the Princeton endowment. The 3.2 percent "floor" on spending is reached when the stabilization fund is less than 5 percent of full value.

The stabilization fund is built up during those years in which total return exceeds 5 percent plus the spending rate and is depleted during years in which total return is smaller. For example, if the stabilization fund is over 50 percent of full value, so that the spending rate is 4 percent, and the total return is 10 percent, then spending is 4 percent, 5 percent is allocated to growth in the endowment, and 1 percent is added to the stabilization fund. The use of a stabilization fund brings spending down automatically if investment results continue below the long-run expectation of 9 percent.

The University of Pennsylvania Formula

The introduction of legislation in Pennsylvania permitting the spending of a portion of realized gains on true endowment as well as income yield led to a proposal by Marshall Blume for a spending rule combining yield and gains.[4] His formula is:

$$\text{Spending in year } T = (R_T{}^* - I_T{}^*) \times V_T{}^*_{-1}$$

In the formula, $R_T{}^*$ is the expected long-run total-return rate on the endowment as of the beginning of the year T, derived, as in Yale's case, through exponential smoothing of past actual rates of return:

$$R_T{}^* = .05\,R_{T-1} + .95\,R_T{}^*_{-1}$$

R_{T-1} is the actual, as opposed to the expected, total-return rate for the year $T-1$. $R_T{}^*_{-1}$ is the long-term total-return rate anticipated as of the beginning of the year $T-1$.

$I_T{}^*$ represents the target growth rate for the endowment, which Blume suggested might be the rate of inflation anticipated by the university's trustees. So $R_T{}^* - I_T{}^*$ is the balance of the expected total-return rate that remains for spending.

$V_T{}^*_{-1}$ is an average market value per unit of the university's Associated Investments Fund at the end of year $T-1$. Again, exponential smoothing is used:

$$V_T{}^*_{-1} = .3\,V_{T-1} + .7\left[V_T{}^*_{-2}(1 + R_T{}^*) - \frac{S_{T-1}}{2}(1 + \sqrt{1 + R_T{}^*}) \right]$$

V_{T-1} is the actual unit value at the end of the year $T-1$; $V_T{}^*_{-2}$ is the averaged, or "smoothed," unit value at the end of the year $T-2$; and S_{T-1} is the spending per unit in the year $T-1$.

Blume suggested setting R^* and I^* at 10 percent and 4 percent initially, so that initial spending would be 6 percent of the smoothed unit value.

Notes

Introduction

[1]National Commission on the Financing of Postsecondary Education, *Financing Postsecondary Education in the United States* (Washington, D.C.: Government Printing Office, December 1973), pp. 53–58. Hereafter cited as National Commission Report.

[2]William Jellema, *From Red to Black?* (San Francisco, Calif.: Jossey-Bass, 1973), p. x. Jellma says,

> This study is important, however, only to the extent that private higher education is important. If diversity and pluralism in higher education are merely words, devoid of real meaning, then these data may be equally devoid of significance.

Frederick Patterson, founder of the United Negro College Fund and president emeritus of Tuskegee Institute, has urged the importance of private institutions as a source of diversity in American higher education. His words are echoed in a report of the Carnegie Commission on Higher Education:

> Private colleges and universities also provide a substantial proportion of the diversity that marks American Higher Education. . . . Many of them reached a peril point in their financing. This should be a source of great public concern.

See Carnegie Commission on Higher Education, *Higher Education: Who Pays? Who Benefits? Who Should Pay?* (New York: McGraw-Hill, 1973), p. 7. Hereafter cited as Carnegie Commission Report.

[3]National Commission Report, Table C-1, pp. 415–419.

[4]Ibid., pp. 194–195.

[5]Ibid., pp. 202–203 and 209.

[6]Carnegie Commission Report, p. 65.

[7]G. Richard Wynn, "Liberal Arts College Pricing: Has the Market Taken Over?", *Liberal Education*, vol. 58, October 1972, pp. 421–432. The importance of tuition level and willingness to pay for quality higher education is examined in detail (on the basis of extensive questionnaires) in Sloan Study Consortium, *Paying for College: Financing Education at Nine Private Institutions* (Hanover, N.H.: University Press of New England, 1974).

[8]*From Red to Black?*, pp. 78–79.

[9]Seymour Harris, *Higher Education: Resources and Finance* (New York: McGraw-Hill, 1962), pp. 423 and 445.

[10]Hans H. Jenny and G. Richard Wynn, *The Golden Years* (Wooster, Ohio: College of Wooster, 1970) and, by the same authors, *The Turning Point* (Wooster, Ohio: College of Wooster, 1972); G. Richard Wynn, *At the Crossroads* (Ann Arbor, Mich.: Center for the Study of Higher Education, School of Education, University of Michigan, 1974).

[11]*Higher Education: Resources and Finance*, p. 457.

[12]National Commission Report, p. 119. Gifts to colleges and universities, per student, showed a decrease of 2.9 percent from 1968–69 to 1973–74, but, after adjusting for inflation, the decrease becomes 25.9 percent. Council for Financial Aid to Education, *Voluntary Support of Education 1973–74* (New York, 1975), p. 5.

Chapter I

[1]James Gilbert Paltridge, Julie Hurst, and Anthony Morgan, *Boards of Trustees: Their Decision Patterns* (Berkeley, Calif.: Center for Research and Development in Higher Education, University of California, Berkeley, 1973), pp. iv–vi.

[2]Carnegie Commission on Higher Education, *The More Effective Use of Resources* (New York: McGraw-Hill, 1972), p. 4. Hereafter cited as Carnegie Report, *Use of Resources*.

[3]Earl F. Cheit, *The New Depression in Higher Education*, a general report for the Carnegie Commission on higher education and the Ford Foundation (New York: McGraw-Hill, 1971), p. 112.

[4]G. Richard Wynn, *Inflation in the Higher Education Industry*, NACUBO Professional File, vol. 6, no. 1 (Washington, D.C.: National Association of College and University Business Officers, January 1975).

[5]Carnegie Report, *Use of Resources*, p. 33.

[6]It is interesting to look at some comments made in 1959 by Beardsley Ruml on academic salaries. In a popular book on the management of liberal arts colleges, he said: "The most serious general problem facing the colleges is the prevailing low level of academic salaries." And he recommended "a wide distribution of competent academic personnel in the salary range of $20,000 to $30,000." Beardsley Ruml and Donald H. Morrison, *Memo to a College Trustee* (New York: McGraw-Hill, 1959), p. 9. The range stated does not look extraordinary at the present time, but translated into 1975 dollars it becomes $36,000 to $54,000.

[7]The reference cited in note 4 describes some procedures for measuring inflation within a particular institution.

[8]Ruml, p. 10.

[9]Carnegie Report, *Use of Resources*, pp. 63–64.

[10]Ibid., p. 45.

[11]Ibid., pp. 40–41.

[12]Ibid., p. 9.

[13]Ibid., pp. 132–133.

[14]Ibid., pp. 107–110.

[15]William B. Bowen, *The Economics of the Major Private Universities* (Berkeley, Calif.: Carnegie Commission on Higher Education, 1968), pp. 10–11. Bowen comments on the effect on instructional costs of attempts by institutions to cover a wider variety of specialized fields, the effect on research costs of improved but more expensive kinds of research, and the heavy costs of preoccupation with public service. The costs of proliferation of courses are recognized in the Carnegie Report (*Use of Resources*, pp. 67–68), with an admonition not only to review the addition of new courses but to see that unnecessary courses are dropped.

[16]Carnegie Report, *Use of Resources*, pp. 119–121.

[17]Ibid., pp. 42–43.

[18]Ibid., pp. 111–112. The growth rate is predicted to decline from about 4.5 percent in 1975 to less than 1 percent in 1981, turning negative in 1982 and falling to minus 2 percent in 1985, then turning less negative and going positive to 1 percent in

1988. These statistics appear to apply only to conventional full-time undergraduate and perhaps graduate enrollment.

[19]Kenneth E. Boulding, "The Management of Decline," an address to the Regents Convocation of the University of the State of New York, Albany, September 20, 1974.

[20]Ruml, pp. 65–67.

[21]Carnegie Report, *Use of Resources*, pp. 17–19.

[22]Wynn, *Inflation in the Higher Education Industry*.

[23]See William F. Massy, *The Economics of Endowed Universities*, Report No. 73-3, Academic Planning Office, Office of the Vice-President and Provost, Stanford University, December 1973.

[24]At a number of institutions, no one knows the proportions of true and quasi endowment, although the requirements of the new American Institute of Certified Public Accountants (AICPA) *Audit Guide* (discussed in Chapter VI) have resulted in serious efforts to make a distinction.

[25]Spending rules, and the Uniform Act, are discussed in Chapter V.

[26]The technicalities of unit values and unit income are discussed in Chapter III.

[27]*Voluntary Support of Education*, 1973–74, is the fifteenth in a series published by the Council for Financial Aid to Education, 680 Fifth Avenue, New York, N.Y. 10019. This edition covers 68 major private universities, 12 private men's colleges, 84 private women's colleges, 442 private coeducational colleges, 64 professional and specialized schools, 217 public institutions, 133 junior colleges, and 313 private secondary and elementary schools. Other statistics are collected by the NACUBO Investment Committee, which reported that for the 128 institutions responding to the June 30, 1974 survey, gift additions to endowment averaged 3.3 percent for the year.

[28]Some of the effects of "nationalizing" universities are discussed in the "Report of the Committee on Private Universities and Private Giving," *University [of Chicago] Record*, April 21, 1973, pp. 95–111.

Chapter II

[1]These observations reflect the opinions of a number of trustees and financial officers. Where several endowment funds are all managed by a single management firm, the performances of the funds often show wide variation, too wide to be explained by the autonomy given to different portfolio managers within the firm. Significant performance differences must be due to the institutions themselves.

[2]A survey by Louis Harris and Associates reported in 1971 that of 214 colleges and universities, 5 percent said that the endowment was the most important responsibility of the trustees, 30 percent said that it was one of the most important, 57 percent said that it was only one of a number of equally important responsibilities, and 8 percent said that it was not a particularly important responsibility. Louis Harris and Associates, Inc., *Managing Endowment Funds: A Survey of Endowed Institutions* (New York: Louis Harris and Associates, Inc., December 1971), p. 45. Hereafter referred to as *Harris Associates Survey*.

[3]Advisory Committee on Endowment Management (Robert Barker, Chairman), *Managing Educational Endowments* (New York: Ford Foundation, 1969; 2d edition, 1972), p. 24. Hereafter referred to as the Barker Report.

[4]A valuable resource to an advisory committee is the Investor Responsibility Research Center, Inc. (1522 K Street, N.W., Washington, D.C., 20005), which prepares detailed analyses of corporate responses to social issues.

[5]This is the arrangement recommended by the Barker Report, p. 38.

[6]In the course of my visits to about 31 institutions during 1968 with John Meck, currently vice-president and chairman of the investment committee of Dartmouth College, it became clear that some trustees and some college and university financial officers (as well as some presidents) were not happy with the traditional makeup of investment committees. Many of these committees appeared to be too large to work

effectively (the Barker Report recommended that the investment committee consist of no more than five or six members), and the selection of committee members was not felt to be good enough.

[7]A number of experienced financial officers have observed that, on occasion, a professional manager will express the greatest pessimism about the economy and the stock market, yet his strategy will continue to favor common stocks. This was especially true in 1974.

[8]Two articles by James L. Farrell, Jr., are particularly helpful: "Analyzing Covariation of Returns to Determine Homogeneous Stock Groupings," *Journal of Business of the University of Chicago*, vol. 47, April 1974, pp. 186–207; and "Homogeneous Stock Groupings, Implications for Portfolio Management," *Financial Analysts Journal*, vol. 31, May–June 1975, pp. 50–62.

[9]Alternatively, a strategy of modest risk but little or no spending, to build up a sizable fund for a future major contribution to the institution, may be called for.

[10]For a description of work at Stanford, see William F. Massy, *The Economics of Endowed Universities*, Report No. 73-3, Academic Planning Office, Office of the Vice-President and Provost, Stanford University, Stanford, California (December 1973).

[11]Appendix 2 presents as examples two statements of investment policy, one from a small college and the other from Harvard University. These are intended not as models to be copied but as an indication of what is being done.

[12]Harris Associates Survey, pp. 47–52. One-third of the 214 institutions reported that they managed their endowments internally, and at two-thirds of these the investment decisions were made by the investment committee. However, fewer than one-third of these committees met as often as once a month.

[13]See note 6.

[14]Harris Associates Survey, pp. 47–50.

[15]Barker Report, p. 26.

[16]There are two possible reasons for this: either none of the trustees knew how well or badly the endowment was performing, or a strong committee chairman made all the decisions and the rest of the committee members were content to leave it all to him.

[17]Two-thirds of the institutions responding to the Harris Associates poll employed an outside manager, someone outside the administration of the college or university. Of the one-third of the institutions that managed their endowments internally, about 20 percent made use of a full-time investment officer on the staff of the institution. And 62 percent made use of a professional investment advisor on a regular basis. (Harris Associates Survey, pp. 54–55.) At least half a dozen institutions have large in-house professional investment staffs.

[18]The substantial use of outside managers is a fairly recent innovation. The Harris Associates Survey (p. 56) reports that, of the colleges and universities turning to outside managers, ". . . 42 percent have gone outside in just the past eight years."

[19]See pp. 165–170.

[20]The Harris Associates Survey (pp. 56–57) found that, of the institutions making use of outside managers, 52 percent gave the manager some discretion. But a significant number of these institutions still specified the mix of investments they wanted (the percentage invested in bonds, stocks, etc.) or the rate of return they were expecting or whether their target was maximum income or capital growth or the kinds of securities they did not want included in their portfolios. And some told their managers to avoid "high-risk" investments.

[21]William L. Cary and Craig B. Bright, *The Law and the Lore of Endowment Funds* (New York: Ford Foundation, 1969).

[22]———, *The Developing Law of Endowment Funds: "The Law and the Lore" Revisited* (New York: Ford Foundation, 1974).

[23]Cary and Bright (1974), p. 13. The thirteen states that had enacted statutes based on the Uniform Act were California, Colorado, Connecticut, Illinois, Kansas, Maine, Maryland, Minnesota, New Hampshire, Tennessee, Vermont, Virginia, and Washington. Subsequently, Delaware, Montana, and North Dakota have joined this group.

[24]Ibid., pp. 48–50.

[25]See also the articles by Farrell mentioned in note 8 above.

[26]John F. Meck, "The Selection of Investment Managers for The Common Fund," paper given June 15, 1971. A summary appears in the "Highlights of the Third Annual Meeting of Members of the Common Fund," September 1974.

[27]An interesting commentary (in the form of "before" and "after" articles) on the careful search for three managers to handle a pension fund, and some of the disappointing results, is instructive with respect to the selection process but does not explicitly blame the competitive approach. Kenneth E. Brunke, Jr., "Inland Steel's Search for a Fund Manager," *Institutional Investor*, vol. 3, December 1969, p. 51; and "Post Mortem on a Split Fund," *Institutional Investor*, vol. 5, August 1971, p. 81.

[28]A discussion of the personalities involved appeared in "Yale's New Partners: Grimm, Ingraham and McNay," *Institutional Investor*, vol. 2, February 1968, p. 23.

[29]Section 501(f) of the Internal Revenue Code.

[30]

FEE SIZE	PERCENTAGE OF INSTITUTIONS
No fee	3
0.1% or less	23
0.1–0.25%	21
0.26–0.75%	21
0.76% or more	10
Flat fee	5
Not sure	17

Source: Harris Associates Survey, p. 75.

[31]Percentage cost, of course, is a function of asset size. When The Common Fund became self-supporting, costs came to over 0.48 percent because the market was declining. According to the data in Forbes 1974 Fund Ratings, the average annual total expense for 62 mutual funds with assets between $100 million and $1 billion was 0.62 percent. *Forbes*, August 15, 1974, pp. 80–94.

The fixed commission rates on stock exchanges which existed until May 1, 1975, and the practice of using directed commissions to pay for various portfolio services make it difficult to know exactly what the costs were for many endowment and mutual funds before that date.

[32]Harold A. Davidson, "College Endowment Fund Management," *Financial Analysts Journal*, vol. 27, January–February 1971, pp. 69–73.

[33]The NACUBO data show an average total return of 7.80 percent a year for 50 endowment funds for the decade 1958–67.

[34]Harris Associates Survey, p. 29.

[35]J. Peter Williamson, *Performance Measurement and Investment Objectives for Educational Endowment Funds* (New York: The Common Fund, 1972), pp. 42–44.

Chapter III

[1]For a fuller discussion of performance measures, see J. Peter Williamson, *Performance Measurement and Investment Objectives for Endowment Funds* (New York: The Common Fund, 1972), hereafter referred to as *Performance Measurement*.

[2]The 1974 edition of *College and University Business Administration* (Washington, D.C.: National Association of College and University Business Officers, 1974), has endorsed the practice, as has the *Audit Guide* for colleges and universities. See Chapter VI.

[3]*Measuring Investment Results by the Unit Method* (New York: Ford Foundation, 1975).

[4]See *Performance Measurement*, pp. 17–21.

[5]The fine points of this calculation and the difference between time-weighted and dollar-weighted rates of return are explored in comfortable detail in *Performance Measurement*, pp. 18–19.

[6]A more precise calculation yields 1.489 percent. $100 \times (1.01489)^2 = 103$. See also *Performance Measurement*, pp. 24–27.

[7]Ibid.

[8]The mean absolute deviation is recommended by the Bank Administration Institute. *Measuring the Investment Performance of Pension Funds* (Park Ridge, Ill.: Bank Administration Institute, 1968).

[9]This might be done just as I calculated efficiency in those examples, by dividing the risk measure, here the volatility, into the excess return. In this case, however, the excess return is usually calculated not as the excess of the average return earned by the fund over the risk-free rate but as the excess of the particular return the fund would be expected to earn when the Index earns the risk-free rate, over the risk-free rate. For the University of Rochester endowment, if we assume a 6 percent risk-free rate over the decade, when the Standard & Poor's 500 Index earned this rate the endowment earned (reading from the line in Figure 3-3) 10 percent, the excess return was then 4 percent, and dividing by the volatility of 1.01 gives a volatility related efficiency of 4.0. For Fund E11, the excess return was 7.2 percent and the efficiency was 1.3. So the University of Rochester endowment was the more efficient. Both were more efficient than the Standard & Poor's 500 Index itself, for which the volatility related measure of efficiency is always zero.

Fund E11 is better diversified, of course, than the University of Rochester endowment, so that this comparison ignores a component of the total variability in the latter. Using standard deviation as the variability measure, we get efficiency measures for E11 and the University of Rochester endowment of $(0.063-0.06)/0.168=0.02$ and $(0.090-0.06)/0.2095=0.14$, respectively.

[10]Calculation of volatility requires the use of a market index, and although Standard & Poor's 500 Index is probably appropriate for deducing the market-related risk in a broadly diversified common stock portfolio, other portfolios will call for other indexes—a bond index, for example, or perhaps a growth stock index.

[11]The efficiency measures also may fail to identify truly superior management. But whether this is the fault of the measures or simply reflects the extreme difficulty of finding any truly superior management is hard to determine. One must treat these measures as approximate, despite their seeming precision, but no other measures appear any better for identifying superior management.

[12]More refined performance measures can be used to identify more narrowly defined objectives and managerial skills. I referred in Chapter II to the stock classification and manager selection methods of Démarche Associates and to two articles on the subject by James Farrell. Performance measures are a part of the methodology.

[13]The use of commissions to buy services is discussed in Chapter II. Some very useful aggregate statistics on pension fund and similar fund performances are published by A.S. Hansen, Inc., and by Dreher, Rogers and Associates, Inc., in New York.

[14]A recent article comments on these weaknesses in performance-measurement services, noting that even size is not always controlled and that different services come up with rather different average performance figures. John Appleton, "Performance Measurements Have Their Limitations," *Pensions and Investments*, February 3, 1975.

[15]The Common Fund is described in detail in Chapter II. Some performance data are given in that chapter (Figure 2-1) and above in this chapter. Data for The Common Fund are available quarterly and show performance on a monthly basis.

[16]Over 150 colleges and universities participate in the annual surveys.

[17]These tests were run by the author. The rank correlation coefficient was −0.05. For a perfect correlation (rankings the same for each fund in each period) the correlation would be 1.0. For a perfect inverse correlation (first-period rankings reversed in second period) the correlation would be − 1.0. A correlation of 0 would indicate no relationship between the two rankings.

[18]The correlation in this was −0.12.

[19]The rank correlation coefficient was 0.67. The correlation between rankings based on rate of return alone was −0.38, which is not surprising because, since the market was

up over the first five-year period and down over the second period, the most volatile funds would have been the most profitable over the first period and the least profitable over the second.

[20]The rank correlation coefficient was 0.18.

[21]The rank correlation coefficient was 0.26.

[22]Lawrence Fisher and James H. Lorie, "Rates of Return on Investments in Common Stock: the Year-By-Year Record, 1926–65," *Journal of Business of the University of Chicago*, vol. 41, July 1968, pp. 291–316.

[23]Roger G. Ibbotson and Rex A. Sinquefield, "Stocks, Bonds, Bills, and Inflation: The Past and the Future," paper presented at the Seminar on the Analysis of Security Prices, Center for Research in Security Prices, Graduate School of Business, University of Chicago, May and November 1974.

[24]See, for example, Michael Jensen, "The Performance of Mutual Funds in the Period 1945–1964," *Journal of Finance*, vol. 23, May 1968, pp. 389–416.

[25]Jack L. Treynor and Kay Mazuy, "Can Mutual Funds Outguess the Market?", *Harvard Business Review*, vol. 44, July–August 1966, pp. 131–136; and J. Peter Williamson, "Measurement and Forecasting of Mutual Fund Performance: Choosing an Investment Strategy," *Financial Analysts Journal*, vol. 28, November–December 1972, p. 78.

Chapter IV

[1]Seymour Harris, *Higher Education: Resources and Finance* (New York: McGraw-Hill, 1962), pp. 423–426, and 479–484.

[2]William K. Cary and Craig B. Bright, *The Developing Law of Endowment Funds: "The Law and the Lore" Revisited* (New York: Ford Foundation, 1974), p. 10.

[3]The real rate of interest was close to zero, the liquidity and default premium, which one earned by moving to less liquid corporate bonds, was 1 to 3 percent, and the risk premium, which one earned by moving on to common stocks, was about 5 to 6 percent. Other studies have suggested a little higher rate of real interest, maybe 2 to 3 percent, and a lower risk premium.

[4]A careful comparison of stocks and bonds over a variety of time periods since 1926 can be found in Stanford Calderwood, "Bonds vs. Equities—Revisited," working paper of Endowment Management and Research Corporation (February 24, 1975).

[5]The Standard & Poor's Index is used to derive a rate of return for the common stocks, the Salomon Brothers high-grade, long-term bond index for the bonds, and 90-day treasury bill rates for the short-term securities.

[6]See Chapter II. Examples of the use of computer simulations to test the effect of combinations of spending policies and investment strategies can be found in J. Peter Williamson, *Performance Measurement and Investment Objectives for Educational Endowment Funds* (New York: The Common Fund, 1972), and in the forthcoming publication, Richard M. Ennis and J. Peter Williamson, *Spending Policy for Educational Endowments* (New York: The Common Fund, 1975).

[7]Probably the best and most readable exposition of the efficient market argument can be found in Lorie and Hamilton, *The Stock Market: Theories and Evidence* (Homewood, Ill.: Richard D. Irwin Inc., 1973). See especially Chapter 4 ("The Efficient Market Hypothesis") and Chapter 5 ("Implications of the Efficient Market Hypothesis").

[8]Common stocks are generally more profitable than short-term investments, and moving back and forth incurs brokerage expenses. Being right half the time leads to a rate of return per year 4 percent *below* the return on an all common stock portfolio. See William F. Sharpe, "Likely Gains from Market Timing," *Financial Analysts Journal*, vol. 31 (March–April 1975), pp. 60–69.

[9]Frank K. Reilly, Ralph E. Smith, and Glenn L. Johnson, "A Correction and Update Regarding Individual Common Stocks as Inflation Hedges," Research Paper

No. 46, College of Commerce and Industry, University of Wyoming (November 1974). This work updated the article "A Note on Common Stocks as Inflation Hedges—The After-Tax Case," *The Southern Journal of Business*, vol. 7 (November 1972), pp. 101–106.

[10]John Lintner, "Inflation and Security Returns," *Journal of Finance*, vol. 30 (May 1975), pp. 259–280.

[11]One of the best and clearest reports on this research is William P. Yohe and Denis S. Karnosky, "Interest Rates and Price Level Changes, 1952–69," *Review of the Federal Reserve Bank of St. Louis*, vol. 52 (December 1969), pp. 18–38.

[12]William L. Cary and Craig B. Bright, *The Law and the Lore of Endowment Funds* (New York: Ford Foundation, 1969), p. 57.

[13]*Harvard College v. Amory*, 26 Mass. 446, 441 (1830).

[14]Some details of the suit are given in Nancy Belliveau, "Is Discretionary Management of Pension Funds in Jeopardy?" *Pensions*, vol. I, no. 2 (Spring 1972), p. 47.

[15]John E. Horner, "Hanover Adopts Aggressive Investment Policies," *College and University Business Administration*, vol. 45 (October 1968), p. 61.

[16]35 N.Y. 2d 512, 364 NY Supp 2d 164 (1974).

[17]Ibid., at 517, 168.

Chapter V

[1]The survey was made by the author and John F. Meck, vice-president and chairman of the investment committee of Dartmouth College, in 1968, to prepare a background study for the Ford Foundation's Barker Report.

[2]Cary and Bright, *The Law and the Lore of Endowment Funds* (New York: Ford Foundation, 1969), p. 9.

[3]Ibid., p. 7.

[4]*Harvard College v. Amory*, 26 Mass. 446, 461 (1830).

[5]Advisory Committee on Endowment Management, *Managing Educational Endowments* (New York: Ford Foundation, 1969; 2d ed. 1972).

[6]Cary and Bright, *Law and Lore*, p. 7.

[7]Harvard still spends no more than income yield on true endowment, but its overall strategy calls for matching current spending to long-run earnings and long-run needs. As a result, for many years Harvard spends less than income yield, reinvesting the balance.

[8]Yale Annual Report 1965–66, pp. 7–8.

[9]Louis Harris and Associates, *Managing Endowment Funds: A Survey of Endowed Institutions* (New York: Louis Harris and Associates, Inc., December 1971), pp. 35–36.

[10]Cary and Bright, *Law and Lore*, p. 12.

[11]For certain kinds of endowment funds—funds dedicated to student aid for example—it might be argued that the institution holds the funds "in trust" for others—for future students in the case of student aid.

[12]Cary and Bright, *Law and Lore*, pp. 42–47.

[13]Citations to most of the statutes can be found in Cary and Bright's second report, *The Developing Law of Endowment Funds: "The Law and the Lore" Revisited* (New York: Ford Foundation, 1974) pp. 12–18.

[14]Most institutions will discourage this form of gift because it forces a return to the old spending rule. But in some instances, it may protect trustees hard pressed by the administration and by faculty, students, or employees to spend currently more than they deem prudent.

[15]Cary and Bright, *"Law and Lore" Revisited*.

[16]Ibid., pp. 9–10.

[17]Richard Ennis and J. Peter Williamson, *Spending Policy for Educational Endowments* (New York: The Common Fund, 1975).

[18]It may be more useful to estimate the long-run total return on an endowment fund in deflated or real terms rather than to try to make separate estimates of the rate

of return and of the rate of inflation in the economy. But in either case, the end result is a spending rate that can be expected to maintain level purchasing power.

[19]Richard Ennis and J. Peter Williamson, *Spending Policy.*

Chapter VI

[1]A number of suggestions for achieving better communication with respect to the handling of investments are contained in *Reporting on Investments of Endowment Funds*, prepared by the investment committee of the National Association of College and University Business Officers.

[2]"Report of the Committee on Accounting Practice of Not-For-Profit Organizations," *The Accounting Review*, Supplement to vol. 46 (1971), pp. 81–163.

[3]Harold Bierman, Jr., and Thomas R. Hofstedt, "University Accounting: Alternative Measures of Ivy League Deficits," Cornell University, unpublished working paper (April 1973).

[4]Committee on College and University Accounting and Auditing, *Industry Audit Guide: Audits of Colleges and Universities* (New York: American Institute of Certified Public Accountants, Inc., 1973). The 1974 edition of *College and University Business Administration* (Washington, D.C.: National Association of College and University Business Officers, 3d ed., 1974), affirms the principles of the *Audit Guide.*

[5]Bierman and Hofstedt, "University Accounting."

[6]The *Audit Guide* entirely avoids the use of surplus or deficit, hence the specific reporting that Bierman and Hofstedt criticized. But it does (as must any set of accounting standards) produce a bottom line, which happens to be the net increase in fund balances. It was not intended to be a single, overall measure of financial strength or performance; indeed, there is no such measure.

[7]Committee on College and University Accounting and Auditing, *Audit Guide*, p. vii.

[8]Ibid., inside front cover.

[9]Ibid., p. 8.

[10]Ibid., p. 9.

[11]*Reporting on Investments of Endowment Funds* discusses the reporting of investment performance in considerable detail.

[12]Committee on College and University Accounting and Auditing, *Audit Guide*, p. 55.

[13]Ibid.

[14]Ibid., p. 17.

[15]*College and University Business Administration*, pp. 147–148.

[16]Committee on College and University Accounting and Auditing, *Audit Guide*, pp. 39–40.

Appendix 1

[1]Robert L. Kaiser, executive secretary for Bequest and Estate Planning of Dartmouth College, kindly supplied much of the information in this appendix.

[2]The *Guide to the Administration of Charitable Remainder Trusts*, published by the Council for Advancement and Support of Education, One Dupont Circle, N.W., Suite 600, Washington, D.C. 20036, provides very detailed information, including sample trust instruments and worksheets for calculating charitable deductions.

[3]The Committee on Gift Annuities, at 1865 Broadway, New York, N.Y. 10023, is an association of representatives of 750 institutions offering gift annuities. (The institutions with the largest gift annuity programs are religious organizations.) The committee has its own actuarial resources and publishes uniform gift annuity rates. It also holds triennial conferences and distributes materials useful in the operation of a gift annuity plan.

[4]Treasury Regulations, § 1.170A-1(d) and Revenue Ruling 72-438. A detailed discussion of the tax aspects of gift annuities can be found in Conrad Teitell, "Federal Tax Implications of Charitable Gift Annuities," *New York Law Forum*, vol. 19 (Fall 1973), pp. 269–288.

[5]Multiplying an annuity receipt by the exclusion ratio gives the portion that is a tax-free return of capital. The exclusion ratio is the ratio of the cost to the total of the expected annuity receipts (the annuitants' life expectancy in years multiplied by the annual annuity). Revenue Ruling 72-438 and Treasury Regulations § 1.72-9.

[6]See Teitell, "Federal Tax Implications."

[7]Ibid.

[8]Ibid.

[9]A further advantage lies in the provision that the charitable deduction is based on the ages of the annuitants at the time payment of the annuity begins rather than at the time of the gift.

[10]The relevant Internal Revenue Code sections are 170(f) (for charitable deductions) and 664 (defining charitable remainder trusts). Treasury Regulation §1.664 is important, as is Revenue Ruling 72-395. Code section 642(c)(5) applies to pooled income funds, as do Regulations §1.642(c)-5, -6, and -7 and Revenue Ruling 72-196.

[11]The unitrust takes over the cost basis of the donor when appreciated assets are used to establish the trust. This is the usual basis carryover rule for gifts under Code section 1015.

[12]Revenue Ruling 60-370.

[13]Treasury Regulations §1.642(c)-5(b)(3).

[14]Internal Revenue Code, §170(f)(4), and Treasury Regulations §1.170A-7, and A-12.

Appendix 3

[1]Institutions have sometimes worried over making the choice between a special and a general nominee. Transactions are better hidden from curious eyes if a general nominee is used, but benefits from dividend over payments (discussed later) are last. Some institutions use special and some use general nominees.

Appendix 4

[1]Data were collected from half a dozen universities with large short-term investments, in the expectation that these institutions would probably work hard at managing these investments and would achieve relatively high rates of return. The average rate of return (weighted by the sizes of the funds) was 5.6 percent a year for the period July 1, 1969, to June 30, 1972. Over this period, the annual average returns of major bank short-term pools ranged from about 6.5 to 8 percent.

Appendix 5

[1]Seymour Harris refers to security lending by the University of Chicago in his book, *Higher Education: Resources and Finance* (1962), p. 491.

Appendix 6

[1]Rates of total return on the PRISA pooled real estate fund (described later in this appendix), deduced from published unit values, were:

Year	1971	1972	1973	1974
Rate	5.3%	5.9%	9.2%	8.8%

[2]Section 511 of the Internal Revenue Code imposes the regular corporate tax rates on unrelated business taxable income of charitable organizations, including colleges and universities. "Unrelated trade or business" is defined in Section 513 as an activity not substantially related to an institution's charitable or educational function. (The fact that the activity produces vital revenue does not prevent it from being unrelated.) Section 512 describes the calculation of unrelated business taxable income, and Section 514(a) states that in the calculation the institution must include with respect to each debt-financed property, as an item of gross income from unrelated trade or business, the same percentage of total gross income as average acquisition indebtedness of the adjusted basis of the property acquired through the indebtedness. Section 514(b) defines "debt-financed property" as any property held to produce income and with respect to which there is acquisition indebtedness, which is in turn defined in Section 514(c) as the unpaid indebtedness incurred in acquiring or improving the property.

Appendix 7

[1]A number of statutes and court decisions apparently prohibit the writing of call options on trust funds. In one opinion, these prohibitions are based on a misunderstanding of call option writing. See Sheen T. Kassouf, "Toward a Legal Framework for Efficiency and Equity in the Securities Markets," *Hastings Law Journal*, vol. 25 (January 1974), pp. 417–434. In July 1974, the comptroller of the currency indicated that he would not criticize the writing of call options by national banks on securities held in trust accounts where the transaction was appropriate for the account. The Internal Revenue Service, as of mid-1975, is still considering whether the writing of call options "jeopardizes the carrying out of charitable purposes" of private foundations, under Section 4944 of the Internal Revenue Code. If it does, the activity will bring about a penalty tax. The Insurance Department of the State of New York has authorized the sale of exchange-traded covered call options by insurance companies, as well as closing purchases (Section 174 of Title 11 of the Official Compilation of Codes, Rules and Regulations, January 1, 1975). The Illinois insurance director has authorized the purchase of exchange-traded call options, as well as the sale of covered options (Departmental Rule 8.02, May 15, 1974). The State of Connecticut has by statute authorized the state treasurer to sell call options.

[2]Revenue Ruling 66–47.

[3]Fischer Black and Myron Scholes, "The Valuation of Option Contracts and a Test of Market Efficiency," *Journal of Finance* (May 1972), pp. 399–417.

Appendix 8

[1]PL 93–406, 1974.

[2]*Conference Report,* Report No. 93–1280, U.S. House of Representatives, 93d Cong., 2d Sess., 1974.

Appendix 9

[1]The adjustment is discussed in detail in Chapter 3 of Richard Ennis and J. Peter Williamson, *Spending Policy for Educational Endowments* (New York: The Common Fund, 1975).

[2]The formula is discussed in detail in the Yale Treasurer's Report for 1966–67.

[3]James M. Litvack, Burton G. Malkiel, and Richard E. Quandt, *A Plan for the Definition of Endowment Income,* Research Memorandum No. 15 (Princeton, N.J.: Financial Research Center, Department of Economics, Princeton University, 1973).

[4]Marshall E. Blume, *An Analysis of Spending Rules for the University's Endowment* (Philadelphia, Pa.: Rodney L. White Center for Financial Research, The Wharton School, University of Pennsylvania, 1973).